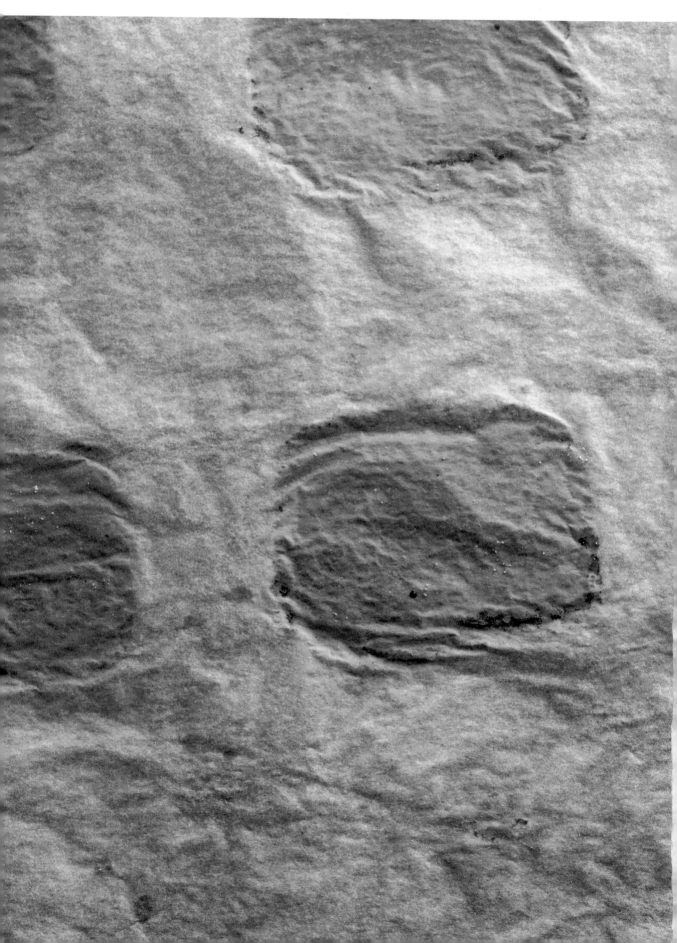

bourke street bakery

the ultimate baking companion

paul allam & david mcguinness

bourke street bakery

the ultimate baking companion

paul allam & david mcguinness

MURDOCH BOOKS

contents

the birth of a bakery

Bourke Street Bakery evolved in a beaten-up old car. Two friends talking about their dreams and aspirations makes for a long drive. David and I spent six months driving around Sydney looking for the perfect site. Somewhere between hours on the road punctuated by 'eating research breaks', we began testing recipes. We discovered we had similar ideas, tastes and opinions.

Our vision of the perfect bakery was small, rustic, homely and timeless; we wanted to create a bakery people would feel comfortable in and make food that people wanted to buy every day. Most importantly, it had to appeal to the whole community. We kept the focus on the quality of ingredients rather than the aesthetic. We were both former chefs who had dabbled in bread and pastry. David had more experience in pastry and I had more in bread, so the demarcation of duties was obvious.

After many false starts, we finally found the site at 633 Bourke Street in Surry Hills, Sydney. Bourke Street Bakery is blessed with incalculable charm and character, which is only enhanced by its positioning close to the local methadone clinic and housing commission high-rise butting up against restaurants, artists and gentrified streets. It was the perfect site and we owe a debt to its previous inhabitants, Crissy and J.C., for selling their space to us and allowing us to live our dream.

Our first sale was a pan au raisin and a bear claw. It was just past 7 am on Tuesday 5 July 2004. We were not yet tired, although that would come; we just felt the fear and excitement of the unknown and the inevitable responsibility of starting a new business. As it turned out, this was the only day we could recall of that first six months. And so started the 'big blur'.

David and I worked from 4 am to 9 pm every day. In the few hours we spent with our respective partners each week, we fought constantly. Selfishly, it seemed not to matter. Each day was better than the last, but even so it was a vicious cycle. We wanted the bakery to be a success, yet every extra sale placed a strain to produce more. We were too paranoid to let just anyone make the product and were also distrustful of our success. We were scared to put on more staff and pay wages, so we raged ahead with what seemed to be a social experiment to test whether two men can happily co-exist in a bakery seventeen hours a day.

We made it through the tough times, but one year on we were running out of space and David took his pastry production elsewhere. So was born Bourke Street Bakery on Broadway. We produced and swapped bread and pastry early in the morning for about a year. Both shops were booming and we started looking for a third, bigger and more sustainable, space where we could reunite our products. This happened in Alexandria; bread and pastry happily co-existed for two years. Then, predictably, arguments started to occur over the mixer, scales and bench. Space in the coolroom was hot property and rather than descend into some sort of primordial chaos, we realised it was once again time for pastry to leave. In the summer of 2008, pastry marched out to Marrickville. The valuable extra space allowed us to extend our range.

The growth of Bourke Street Bakery has been totally organic. We had no grand plan on that first day. We took our time. We did it well. We stayed true to our product. We have never had marketing or PR people involved. We have always felt that we needed to turn each person who walks through the door into a PR machine. And to do that, we make sure the product is damn good. Simple really.

When we go to round up the people who helped us in those first days, weeks and months, it's the usual suspects of family and friends who deserve the most thanks. The success of Bourke Street Bakery and the culmination of all our wonderful recipes in this book would not have been possible without our chef friends who worked the odd day, Dave's brother who did the carpentry work, my sister who chose our infamous brown exterior, our wives who served and washed and smiled at us like we were lost, our good friend Dan, who offered counsel and coffee in equal measures. My in-laws, who probably represented half the takings on any given day, and also my parents, who made the shelves and cushions for the shop, and would have made anything really, I only had to ask.

And, most importantly, a big thank you to all of our customers who continue to support us at Bourke Street and beyond.

Thank you

Paul Allam

about this book

Baking is part science, part stoneground milling and part river-running romance. But it's not the romance that will keep your baking consistently good, it's the science. That's not to say you should not feel a deep connection to the earth. At Bourke Street Bakery we buy organic flour directly from a stoneground mill. If you take out our electric deck oven and mixer from the production process, you are not far away from how bakeries would have operated in the 16th century.

Hopefully, with good-quality ingredients and a little technique, the rest of the baking process will take care of itself. A good pair of scales and an electric mixer are indispensable when baking. We have tested and retested these recipes but allowances still have to be made for the equipment and experience of each baker — not every mixer is the same; climate is a large variable in any commercial bakery, let alone a domestic kitchen; and the oven, or more to the point, its thermostat, can vary greatly.

If your first attempt doesn't look exactly like the pictures in this book, don't give up. Think about why it didn't turn out and you'll have a greater chance of fixing the problem next time and becoming a better baker. When you think you have isolated the problem, just change that one component. Try not to change too many things at once so that ultimately you can understand the process and learn from your mistakes. This can be a slow but necessary part of becoming a good baker and as you will quickly discover, the results make the effort well worthwhile.

before you begin

For any baker, and in particular a home baker, creating something from scratch is a beautiful thing. Being able to share your creation is a double pleasure. Baking at home for yourself or your loved ones is always going to be well received. No matter what the outcome you can be sure that anything you make is going to be much fresher than what you can purchase in a supermarket.

As in any trade, knowing how to work your tools and equipment is as important as the method. Baking is no different — your tools may be your bare hands and your equipment flour, water, yeast and butter, but it is no less important knowing how they should act and react.

ingredients

This book is best used in the spirit of Bourke Street Bakery: try not to worry too much about the look of the product. Worry about where you are going to get the ingredients: flour, butter, salt. Making sure you start with the best-quality ingredients you can find will ensure a superior end result.

flour

Flour is the most important ingredient you will need as a baker. To understand flour, you need to understand the common wheat kernel. As this book is not meant to be a textbook, but a helpful overview for the home baker, let's keep it brief and simple.

Within the wheat kernel there are three main parts: bran, endosperm and germ. The bran is the outer layer and contains B vitamins and dietary fibre. The endosperm is the largest part of the wheat kernel, comprising most of the protein and starch. The germ, or the sprouting section, contains the oils and fats.

Modern technology means that machines can now de-bran the wheat kernel. This leaves just the endosperm and germ to be milled; generally, the germ is then separated as it contains a lot of oil and fat that will shorten the shelf-life of the flour. The strength of flour is dependent on its protein percentage and this can be as variable as the strain or type of wheat sown.

For example, to get wholemeal flour, the whole kernel is milled, which results in a shorter shelf-life as the flour contains a lot of oils and fat from the germ and bran. Bran also has a shorter shelf-life because the outer layer, containing oils, is milled. To get white flour, only the endosperm is milled, as it contains most of the starch and protein and only a little of the oils and fat. White flour will have a higher protein percentage and a longer shelf-life.

When you buy a packet of wheatgerm, the germ has been separated and milled, meaning it will be extremely good for you as it contains a lot of nutrients, oils and fats. The next time you dig into a bowl of tabouli and notice how great the cracked wheat is, just think that the whole wheat kernel has been de-branned and then crushed to complement the tabouli.

The different types of flours in the supermarket result from blending and can mean adding more protein to create high-protein flour, removing protein to create cake flour or removing some of the germ or bran to produce a lighter wholemeal flour.

In the production of generic white refined flour, much of the goodness is lost. One of the main reasons for this is the high speed of the milling process, which creates a lot of heat and kills many nutrients and enzymes. Another enemy of goodness is bleaching, whereby flour is artificially bleached to help the gluten stretch more. This process is unnecessary, as the flour will bleach naturally if left to sit for a couple of weeks, but it is often done to keep up with the supply and demand of the busy marketplace.

When baking bread, you generally want an organic flour, which by nature is hard or strong, with a high protein percentage. This is best purchased from health food stores or from bakeries such as ours (we will happily sell you flour). As a home baker you should make the effort to source the best flour possible. Good organic flour will mean your loaves have the potential to be bigger and more flavoursome than if using cheaper, inferior flour. If you are going to commit to spending the time developing and nurturing a starter for a sourdough, you should also commit to finding the best flour you can.

On the other hand, when baking cakes or making pastry, you want to use soft flour. This is flour with a low protein percentage. With cakes, there is no need to mix and stretch the gluten to create an elastic dough. Plain (all-purpose) flour is the best option as it is a low-protein flour that will leave your product soft and crumbly, a texture which is desirable for most cakes.

Having said that, organic plain flour will often have too high a protein percentage and can restrict the rising agents within your recipe. Organic plain flour has a beautiful deep earthy flavour, which you may not want in a cake — you do not want the flour to overpower the other flavours. However, that also works in the reverse when you are making a cake that would benefit with the flavour of an organic flour — this is a matter of taste and personal preference and can be refined with practice.

All the flour used to make the sourdough loaves at Bourke Street Bakery is sourced from a certified organic stoneground mill. The slow process of stone grinding means there is little heat generated and little goodness lost. Of course, this is not always going to be an option for the home baker, so our advice is to keep it simple — try and find a reliable producer that you can trust to source your (preferably organic) flour.

salt

When baking bread and making croissant dough, salt serves a couple of important functions. It imparts flavour and it acts as a stabiliser, stopping the yeast proving too quickly. In cakes, the salt is weighed to balance the sugar and other additives.

When baking bread it is best to use sea salt, which will be organic, unrefined and have a better flavour. You will not need to crush sea salt flakes, as they will break down in the dough naturally. Rock salt will be too intense and the crystals will be too large and will have trouble breaking down within the dough. When making pastry, it is best to use good old-fashioned cooking salt as the crystals will dissolve easily into any mix and the potency will be consistent.

water

At home, using bottled water for baking is a possibility. At Bourke Street Bakery we cannot, so we use filtered tap water instead. Another option is to allow a bucket of tap water to sit ambient overnight; some of the impurities within will disperse. Using water straight from the tap is also fine, just not as good as the above options. When creating a starter for a sourdough it is safer to use bottled water in much the same way as you would take care of a newborn and avoid feeding it any impurities.

Water temperature is also an important factor when baking. Most of our doughs at Bourke Street Bakery need to come out of the mixer at 26°C (79°F), which means that you need to alter the water temperature depending on the season. Altering the water temperature is the easiest way to alter the dough temperature. Generally speaking, when making pastry you will need to use chilled water, as you want the butter to crumble into the flour, not melt into it.

butter

Butter is as important for making pastry as flour is for bread. At Bourke Street Bakery we have always imported butter from Europe; first from Denmark and now from Belgium. We always use unsalted butter. There is no modern use for salted butter, as salt was only added to butter to prolong its shelf-life. These days most people have refrigerators so that is not a concern. Controlling the amount of salt in anything you cook is important.

Butter has different fat contents and different flavours but most importantly it has different roles depending on whether you are making croissants or other kinds of pastry. A pure and simple product like the croissant relies on good butter — without it, your croissant will be substandard. So, if you are making croissants at home, use good European butter.

When making other kinds of pastry, however, butter is used in a different manner. Generally speaking, butter with a high water content, which is typical of most cheap butters from the supermarket, will make your pastry light and flaky. In this instance, it is best to use a cheaper butter that has a low fat content and consequently a high water content.

It is interesting to note that at one time at Bourke Street Bakery we were not able to import the Danish butter (with an 80 per cent fat content) that we had grown to love. Having no choice, we switched to another butter with a 99 per cent fat content instead. This turned out to be catastrophic and resulted in croissants that were too rich and oily. So you can see the increased purity of any ingredient is not always an advantage.

commercial yeast

At Bourke Street Bakery we use commercially made compressed fresh yeast, which is a living one-celled fungus with a life span. Using fresh yeast every day keeps us ahead of the use-by dates for our breads. For home bakers, dried yeast is an easier and more convenient option most of the time, although we still recommend using fresh yeast whenever possible. You will need to check the use-by dates on both fresh and dried yeast. If you use active dried yeast instead of fresh, you will need to halve the amount used in the ingredient list and hydrate it with warm water, using about 10% of the water from the recipe, before adding to the other ingredients.

Fresh yeast needs to be kept wrapped in the packaging it comes in and stored in the refrigerator — as it needs to breathe, wrapping tightly in plastic wrap would be detrimental to its survival. Generally, fresh yeast will have a life span of one month, although it loses strength as time passes. Fresh or dried yeast serves the same function as a starter (see pages 40–5). Effectively, they convert sugar into carbon dioxide, which helps to make a loaf rise, but the pre-made dried yeasts just do it more quickly.

There are more and more types of dried yeast available on supermarket shelves, in health food stores and in beer-brewing shops. Many of our recipes require a long slow prove to develop flavour and texture. Active dried yeast is better for baking purposes, as instant dried yeast just works too quickly. Instant dried yeast used in our recipes would mean the dough would over-prove before you had time to bake the loaf. Dried yeast lasts for months and even longer if kept in the refrigerator or freezer.

equipment

For many of us, walking into a kitchenware store is a
therapeutic retail experience (for some of us a habit!) and it
is impossible to escape without buying another 'must have'
product. To be a good baker, you do not need to have every
piece of kitchen equipment ever invented — it will just end
up cluttering your kitchen. However, we can recommend
the following items to help you in the kitchen and make
the baking process, and ultimately the pleasure of eating,
better all round.

scales

A good set of electronic scales is the most important piece of equipment
a home baker can own. You can get reliable small scales from any decent
kitchenware or specialty store. An electronic scale with a 5 kilogram (11 lb)
maximum and increments of no more than 2 grams is a good option. For the
best results always weigh each ingredient. We use grams as the prime source
of measurement in the bakery as it provides the most consistent and accurate
outcome. A gram is a gram anywhere in the world, which cannot be said for
cups. Also, the way you fill or pack a cup or spoon will vary from person
to person. We now live in a digital world, so we recommend using scales for
a superior measure.

electric mixer

An electric mixer is a worthwhile investment if you are a regular baker. The
most important thing to check is that it has a strong motor. The motor drives
the cog that drives the dough hook or paddle attachment. If you overheat the
motor and it burns out, you will generally need to replace the whole mixer.
This can happen if you are often mixing dough with a low water content, as
the dough will be stiff and cause the motor to work extra hard to move the
dough hook around. This is not worth burning out the motor for. If you see
the mixer struggling, and the dough hook is stopping and starting, take the
dough out and finish it by hand.

temperature probe

A temperature probe is a metal spike that has a temperature gauge on the
end. It is a great tool to have when baking to determine the temperature
of a dough. At Bourke Street Bakery the dough comes out of the mixer at

approximately 25°C–27°C (77°F–81°F). Yeast, natural or not, needs warmth to allow the reaction of sugars converting to carbon dioxide, so it is important to have an accurate gauge of temperature.

timer

A timer can also be invaluable in the kitchen. Baking is a game of 'seconds' and it is worth keeping track of these, especially at the mixing or baking stage. Most probably, your mixer and oven will not have great timing mechanisms so it is good to have an accurate timer that is dedicated solely to the purpose of baking.

notebook

A little baking notebook is a great resource as you can only learn from your mistakes if you can remember them. Writing down anything about what you have achieved from a mix, prove or bake, or even what you had hoped for or expected, is an important learning tool. Looking back at the notebook the next time you attempt the same recipe should help you eradicate any possible problems.

other kitchen tools

There are also a handful of smaller tools, which can make life a lot easier, especially if you bake regularly. Some of the more common items that you may find handy are:

- a serrated knife or scalpel for scoring
- a scraper for cleaning the flour off your bench
- a divider for dividing the dough into loaves
- an oven temperature dial for double-checking that your oven thermostat is reading correctly
- a solid pair of oven mitts
- a hearth or pizza stone (always place in the oven before baking so that the stone is hot). The aim of baking on the hearth is to supply the loaf with an initial burst of bottom heat, which will make the loaf spring upwards more than if baked on a tray
- a spray bottle for spraying water into the oven
- oil spray for greasing trays and tins
- a heat-resistant spatula
- a natural (not nylon) bristle pastry brush
- a piping (icing) bag — a couple of medium-sized piping bags for savoury and one for sweet recipes is ideal, with a few different-sized nozzle attachments
- two plastic 2–3 litre (70–105 fl oz) buckets for starter cultivation.

breads

basics and techniques

Patience in baking is not a virtue; it is a necessity. A good baker can control the dough if they can control the environment where the dough is created. However, sometimes with baking, as with life, things don't go to plan and you might have to follow the dough instead of leading it. The recipes within this book are a guideline and not a strict doctrine. Bread baking is half science and half wild creation, which is its beauty. If you think a loaf of bread is ready to go in the oven from the techniques you have learnt, but the recipe says hold it back another 10 minutes, throw the little bugger in the oven; trust yourself. The worst that can happen is that you learn a little more from the experience.

Even within a commercial bakery, the baker has to understand the different quirks of an oven or mixer. The trick is to think about how the dough or loaf has changed and why, and then try to understand its relation to the equipment you are using. For example, if the oven is hotter at the back than the front you will need to turn the loaf more frequently. You may also need to think about what the prove is doing to the loaf of bread — it is warming the dough and making it moist, allowing it to rise — and consider any changes you may need to make to alter the proving environment.

At Bourke Street Bakery we do not subscribe to the theory that the better the machine the better the product will be. Having better toys will not make you a better baker. Technique and knowledge, and of course practice, are the only things that will help you to make great bread.

mixing

Gliadin and glutenin are two proteins that exist in flour and when these are mixed they form strands of gluten. The gluten's job is to trap bubbles of carbon dioxide within the elastic dough that will rise up and form a larger structure.

When testing to see if a dough is ready, grab a ball of dough, roll it up and stretch it around your fingers to create a window pane. If this window is translucent and doesn't tear, you have created a well-developed dough. If it tears without even forming a window or struggles to form one, the dough will need further mixing.

If you are mixing by hand you should be safe in the knowledge that it will be very hard to overmix the dough. You can actually mix any dough by hand, but some doughs with higher water percentages, such as pizza and olive oil doughs, can be a little tricky and annoying. Always combine the dough in a bowl with a spoon before tipping the contents onto the bench to start kneading.

To ease the burden, you can mix these doughs in two or three stages, with 5–10 minute breaks in between. This will not only benefit your forearms, but the structure of the dough also improves. You can also spray your bench with a little oil between kneading and scrape down the bench regularly once you get going.

Remember too, that kneading is a technique; senseless violent action will get you nowhere. Use the ball of your hand to create air pockets by pushing down and away while using the other hand to pull the dough over. The gluten and their strands are responsible for trapping air within the dough. It is this trapped air that will allow your loaf to rise into a bigger structure.

If you are using an electric mixer to mix the dough, make sure that the dough is not too big for the bowl. Depending on the capacity of your electric mixer you may need to halve or third the dough recipes. Check the timing mechanism on your mixer with another timer for accuracy and as with hand mixing, regularly scrape the edges of the bowl to incorporate all the ingredients into the mix as you work.

resting/autolyse

With both bread making and pastry there are many stages when you need to 'rest' the dough. This allows time for the gluten strands to relax back to their original position. It is much like a muscle in the body that has been working and then relaxes back to its original resting position — the dough is developing all the time even when it is resting.

Autolyse, sometimes called a hydrated rest, is a term used to describe this resting period after the flour and water have been mixed together, which gives the gluten strands time to bond naturally. At Bourke Street Bakery we mix the starter, flour and water, then allow the dough to have its rest, or autolyse, for 20 minutes before adding salt and mixing the dough again.

Resting the dough before dividing it into shapes is very important to find consistency in shape. For example, when rolling out olive oil dough to cut smaller rolls, the dough must be allowed to rest as a whole before cutting the rolls, so the gluten strands can relax back into their original shape. If you cut the rolls without resting the dough first, the gluten strands will relax back into their original shape, thereby shrinking and distorting the shape of each roll.

bulk prove

There are two main stages of proving — the bulk prove and the final prove. The bulk prove is the stage where the dough has come out of the mixer and is sitting in an oiled bowl or container. The final prove is the stage when the loaves have been shaped and are sitting in a basket or on a tray ready to go into the oven (see page 36). The bulk prove does not need any humidity or high temperatures, a room temperature of 20°C–22°C (68°F–72°F) is fine.

For almost all of the recipes in this book we do long, slow bulk proves that do not require high ambient temperatures. This yields more flavour within the dough before it is divided and a tastier baked loaf.

knocking back the dough

Knocking back a dough is the baker's reaction to the bulk proving period. It is the process where the baker physically folds the dough over into halves or thirds (see the step-by-step guide opposite).

It serves a few purposes. It redistributes the temperature and the yeast's (natural or not) food supply and it activates the gluten strands again after they have relaxed. Knocking back the dough also allows the gas that has built up during the proving period to escape before it breaks the structure of the dough, which in turn allows the dough to develop further and become stronger. The knock back is usually done midway through the bulk prove (the first stage of proving), sometimes more than once. After the dough has been knocked back you will almost always need to continue to prove the dough for a further one hour.

shaping the dough

Once the dough has been knocked back and the bulk prove is complete, you can begin shaping the loaves. When shaping a loaf you are primarily creating tension, as the development, kneading and mixing of the dough has already occurred. Do not knead the dough excessively as you do not want to knock all the air out of the dough. At Bourke Street Bakery we mostly make round loaves or batards. A batard is an oblong-shaped loaf, similar to a baguette, but generally shorter and wider than a baguette.

1. To knock back the dough press the dough out into a rectangle on a lightly floured surface.

2. Visualise the rectangle divided into thirds and fold over the end thirds to overlap in the middle.

3. Start at the edge closest to you and again visualise the dough divided into thirds.

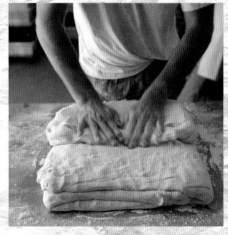

4. Fold one third of the dough over to meet in the middle.

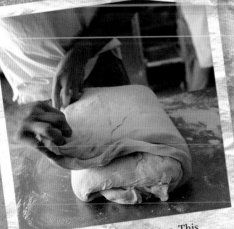

5. Fold the final third over the top. This completes the knock back.

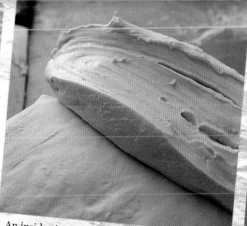

6. An inside view of the dough will clearly show a series of lines — these indicate how layers are created during the knock back.

You will need to divide the dough into the required portions as instructed in each recipe. Working with one portion of dough at a time, place it on a clean work surface; do not flour the surface. Surround the dough with your cupped hands, always keeping your hands in contact with the dough. In an anti-clockwise motion, start rolling the dough to create a tight ball with a smooth surface. Once you have achieved this, place the pre-shaped ball of dough on a lightly floured work surface. Repeat with the remaining dough portions — let the balls of dough rest on the flour for 20 minutes, covered with plastic wrap.

When you are ready to do the final shape you will be required to make either a round loaf or a batard. To shape a round loaf, stretch each dough portion out to double its width. Fold a third into itself towards the middle, then fold in the other third to overlap. Use the ball of your hand to press down on the dough and push outwards, using the resistance of the bench — you do not need to use a lot of force at this stage; all you are doing is creating tension and form. If you are tearing the dough you are using too much force. Roll the ball back and forth with one hand and use your other hand to turn the dough into itself — you may use some flour to facilitate this. You should be left with a tight, smooth ball of dough with a noticeable seam where you have forced the dough to converge. To close the seam, take the top of the ball and place it into the palm of your dominant hand. Turn it so the ball is sandwiched between your two hands and use the little finger of the hand that is not cradling the dough to run over the seam and close it.

To shape a batard (see pictures on pages 34–5), stretch each dough portion out to double its width. Fold a third into itself towards the middle, then fold in the other third to overlap. Then, as if you are building a paper aeroplane, fold it in to create the nose cone at the end furthest from the edge of the bench. Press this down to prevent any large air pockets forming. With your fingers tensed, press down onto the nose cone and fold inwards keeping the action tight — this is called crimping. Use small movements with your fingers, folding the dough over and pressing down as you work to create tension and form. Crimp halfway into the dough, then with the ball of your dominant hand press down against the seam closing it into the dough. Continue this motion with both hands, folding the dough over to close the seam. Check to see that the seam is straight and closed; if not, pinch the seam to close it.

Positioning the seam is an important aspect of shaping the dough. If it is a round loaf you want the seam in the middle of the bottom of the loaf. If it is a baguette or batard, you want a nice straight seam in the middle. Always lay the dough seam side down on the tray when baking as it does have the potential to open up if laid with the seam facing up.

1. To shape a loaf, surround the ball of dough with both cupped hands, keeping your hands in contact with the dough at all times. Roll in an anti-clockwise motion to create tight, smooth balls.

2. Once all the dough has been rolled into balls, let the balls rest on a floured surface covered with plastic wrap for at least 20 minutes.

5. To make a batard loaf, fold the dough in at the end furthest from the edge of the bench to create a nose cone, similar to making a paper aeroplane.

6. Press down onto the nose cone and fold inwards, keeping the action tight.

3. Once the dough has rested, stretch each ball out to double its width so that it is even all over.

4. Fold one-third of the dough towards the middle, then fold the other third over the top. At this stage you can continue to make either a round or batard-shaped loaf. To make a round loaf, turn the dough into itself to create a tight, smooth ball and continue to create tension and form as for Step 7 before closing the seam.

7. Use small movements with your fingers, folding the dough over and pressing down as you work to create tension and form.

8. You need to continue to fold the dough over and use the ball of your dominant hand to close the seam — for a batard loaf it should be straight down the middle.

retarding/final prove

You can prove the bread in either a round or batard-shaped bread basket or banetton. A banetton is a traditional proving basket lined with linen and flour, or if they are cane, just flour. They allow a loaf to conform to a shape and add support during the final prove. To replicate this, line a small basket with a tea towel (dish towel), lightly dust with flour and place the loaf inside, seam side up. If you are using a cane basket, you don't need the tea towel and can simply dust the basket with flour. If you are not using a basket at all, place the loaf on a baking tray lined with baking paper, seam side down, then cover the tray loosely with a plastic bag. Do not use plastic wrap as you want to give the loaf some room to move as it proves, but you must make sure the loaf is covered otherwise it will form a crust.

If you are making a sourdough loaf it will need to go through a retarding stage before the final prove. This is when the dough is placed, in baskets, in the refrigerator for anywhere between 8 and 12 hours. This long slow fermentation allows the bread to develop a lot of its characteristic sourness. If you are making yeasted breads or olive oil breads you do not need to retard the dough and can continue with the final prove.

The final prove is where most home bakers fall down, mainly because it is hard to replicate the conditions you need. The final prove needs to have a climate of 80% humidity and a constant temperature of 25°C–27°C (77°F–81°F). Bread needs warmth to rise and humidity to facilitate that rising. Heat will activate the yeast (natural or not) — which will eat the sugar, creating carbon dioxide, and as a result the dough will 'grow' in size. Heat and humidity are things that you will need to find or create in your kitchen. As a home baker, the best way to achieve a stable proving environment in an open kitchen without a commercial prover is to use a hot electric frying pan filled with water and then placed in a cupboard, cabinet or a tent-like structure made from a bed sheet. If you have a closed kitchen, you can put the oven on to create some heat and a saucepan filled with boiling water to create humidity.

Knowing when to put a loaf into the oven can be tricky, as it is dependent on the environment and the process that has come before. At this stage you should be looking for a few key attributes. Firstly, the loaf should have grown in size by at least one-third but more commonly two-thirds. Second, when the dough is pushed with your finger, it should spring back immediately yet slowly. If it holds the indent too long, does not spring back at all or deflates, the loaf is over-proved. If this is the case, then there is nothing you can do except put it in the oven as soon as possible. Do not score the loaf as it will release the remaining gas that it needs to rise. If you cannot make a proper indent or the dough takes too long to spring back, the loaf is under-proved and you will need to prove it for longer.

1. To score a loaf use a scalpel or small serrated knife — scoring the loaf releases a little gas in the dough and will help to create an appealing shape.

2. When you are scoring a round loaf you can make two cuts, keeping both as deep and long as each other so the loaf rises evenly.

scoring

Scoring or slashing is when you take a knife or scalpel and make an incision into a loaf. Scoring allows the loaf to bloom or rise fully. The incision releases a little bit of the gas inside, so the dough pushes up to fill the void and create an appealing shape. At Bourke Street Bakery, we don't slash all of our loaves nor is it necessary to, especially those with a high water content. Some loaves are slashed before the final prove, allowing the loaf to prove into its slash long before it hits the oven.

The best implement to use to slash or score a loaf is a scalpel. The next best tool is a small serrated knife. There are many styles of slashes; we recommend you keep it simple. Start with a 2 cm (3/4 inch) deep cross or a single line down the centre. Holding the knife at different angles can create varying effects. If you slash straight down into the middle of a loaf holding the knife vertically upright, the loaf will rise up and fill the void symmetrically, without pushing the crust either left or right. If you hold your knife at a 45 degree angle and slash from right to left, the crust will flip over and out, away from where you made the incision, much like a car door opening through the top of the loaf.

baking

Baking really should be the easiest of the big three — mixing, proving, baking. When the loaf is ready to bake, turn it out of its basket onto a baking tray lined with baking paper, seam side down. Remember to preheat the oven according to the directions and then to turn the heat down before putting the loaf in. If you are using a hearth or pizza stone, place it into the oven when you turn it on to heat it up, not when you put the loaf in. Check that your oven's thermostat is reading correctly with an independent oven thermometer and adjust it accordingly.

To create enough moisture in the oven so the loaf can reach its full oven bloom (a loaf's potential growth in the oven), put the loaf in the oven, then close the door leaving just enough room to insert the nozzle of a water spray gun and spray for 10 seconds. Without this moisture the loaf will instantly crust up and not rise any further.

During baking you will always need to turn the loaf around halfway through so that it bakes evenly. If your loaf is on a tray, just turn the tray around. If it is on a hearth stone you need to turn it around with a long pair of tongs. If you are baking four loaves, two to a tray on two shelves, you also need to swap these around as well as turning them.

When the loaf is baked, remove it from the oven with a tea towel and tap the underside. If you hear a hollow sound it is ready. Let it cool a little before cutting into slices and serving — if it has a gooey line at its base once it is cooled and cut, then the loaf is underbaked.

starters

If you mix flour and water in a bowl and let it sit in a warm place, after a few days, a wild yeast is created from bacteria in the flour and air. This wild yeast eats the natural sugars in the flour and converts them into carbon dioxide (creating bubbles) and lactic acid (creating the sourness). Once this process of natural fermentation has begun, we have what is known as a starter. This is the first crucial step in making sourdough bread. Like every living thing a starter needs to be fed and nurtured. You have to make sure the room temperature is fairly constant and keep it away from certain additives, such as salt, sugar, acid or vinegar, which will harm it. The starter needs to be fed once a day with water and flour. Over time, the flavour of the starter becomes stronger and more complex.

There is more than one method to feed and sustain a starter. Some will advocate using a little organic orange juice or grape skins, adding raisins, yoghurt, honey, potato water or malt. The theory is that additives with inherent natural cultures will help to create the wild yeasts a lot more quickly, and the natural sugars within these ingredients will feed the starter and help it grow stronger faster.

Following a daily routine for feeding a white or rye starter will make the process much easier. Try to have a regular time to feed your starter — breakfast is good, as everyone has breakfast. If you live in a warm climate, after the first week, put your starter in the refrigerator overnight for the rest of its life. During the day, you can leave the starter at ambient room temperature, but if it is a particularly hot day, say over 26°C (79°F), keep it in the refrigerator between feeds. As the starter gets hotter it will eat more quickly, run out of food between feeds and start to fade. You will need to lower the temperature of the starter so that it has enough food to grow between meals.

white starter

Below is the white starter recipe we use at Bourke Street Bakery, however any of the ingredients mentioned on page 41 would be fine to add to this recipe. We would advocate using some ripe organic grapes. Use two clean plastic buckets or bowls to mix the starter.

day one
Genesis — work on a ratio of 50% water and 50% flour to starter.
Use a clean bucket and place in it 50 ml (1¾ fl oz) water and 50 g (1¾ oz/⅓ cup) organic plain flour.

day two
First feed — the total weight of the starter is now 100 g (3½ oz). For the first feed, add 50 ml (1¾ fl oz) water and 50 g (1¾ oz/⅓ cup) organic plain flour. Stir the water and flour together with a spoon, then add the starter and fold it through to combine. Cover with plastic wrap and set aside overnight.

day three
Second feed — the total weight of the starter is now 200 g (7 oz). For the second feed, add 100 ml (3½ fl oz) water and 100 g (3½ oz/⅔ cup) organic plain flour. Stir the water and flour together with a spoon, then add the starter and fold it through to combine. Cover with plastic wrap and set aside overnight.

day four
Third feed — the total weight of the starter is now 400 g (14 oz). For the third feed, add 200 ml (7 fl oz) water and 200 g (7 oz/1⅓ cups) organic plain flour. Stir the water and flour together with a spoon, then add the starter and fold it through to combine. Cover with plastic wrap and set aside overnight.

day five
At this stage you need to discard some of the starter, otherwise you will end up with too much starter that is not active enough to use. On day five the total weight of the starter will be 800 g (1 lb 12 oz). You need to reduce the starter weight to 100 g (3½ oz), discarding the rest to the compost.

After the first five days you need to repeat the same first, second and third feeds for a total of three weeks (see weekly feeding schedule, page 44). On week four you need to increase the feeds so that the starter is ready to use in a dough (see final feeding schedule, page 45).

rye starter

Creating a rye starter is similar to creating a white starter, except a lot easier, as the rye flour will ferment more quickly. The guiding principal is the same, with a variation of 60% water to 40% flour — rye flour can absorb a lot more water than white flour, so it needs a little more water to help it rise.

day one
Genesis — Use a clean bucket and place in it 60 ml (2 fl oz/$\frac{1}{4}$ cup) water and 40 g (1$\frac{1}{2}$ oz) organic rye flour. Stir the water and flour together with a spoon. Cover with plastic wrap and set aside overnight.

day two
First feed — the total weight of the starter is now 100 g (3$\frac{1}{2}$ oz). Your first feed will be 60 ml (2 fl oz/$\frac{1}{4}$ cup) and 40 g (1$\frac{1}{2}$ oz) organic rye flour. Stir the water and flour together with a spoon, then add the starter and fold it through to combine. Cover with plastic wrap and set aside overnight.

day three
Second feed — the total weight of the starter is now 200 g (7 oz). The second feed will be 120 ml (3$\frac{3}{4}$ fl oz) water and 80 g (2$\frac{3}{4}$ oz) organic rye flour. Stir the water and flour together with a spoon, then add the starter and fold it through to combine. Cover with plastic wrap and set aside overnight.

day four
Third feed — the total weight of the starter is now 400 g (14 oz). The third feed will be 240 ml (8 fl oz) water and 160 g (5$\frac{3}{4}$ oz) organic rye flour. Stir the water and flour together with a spoon, then add the starter and fold it through to combine. Cover with plastic wrap and set aside overnight.

day five
On day five the total weight of the starter will be 800 g (1 lb 12 oz). You need to reduce the starter weight to 100 g (3$\frac{1}{2}$ oz), discarding the rest to the compost.

Continue to follow the feeding schedules as for the white starter (see charts, pages 44–5) making sure you adjust the feed amounts accordingly. The rye starter will not bubble and froth as much as the white starter. It will rise slowly up, then fall dramatically in on itself when it has run out of sugar to eat and convert into carbon dioxide, so it can not rise any further. This tells you that your starter is active and that it needs to be fed.

white starter weekly feeding schedule
weeks 1–3

	feed time	water	flour	total weight
DAY 1				
	Genesis 7 am	50 ml (1¾ fl oz)	50 g (1¾ oz/⅓ cup)	100 g (3½ oz)
DAY 2				
	First feed 7 am	50 ml (1¾ fl oz)	50 g (1¾ oz/⅓ cup)	200 g (7 oz)
DAY 3				
	Second feed 7 am	100 ml (3½ fl oz)	100 g (3½ oz/⅔ cup)	400 g (14 oz)
DAY 4				
	Third feed 7 am	200 ml (7 fl oz)	200 g (7 oz/1⅓ cups)	800 g (1 lb 12 oz)
DAY 5 *Place 700 g (1 lb 9 oz) of the sourdough starter in the compost.* *Start again to feed 100 g (3½ oz) of sourdough starter.*				
	First feed 7 am	50 ml (1¾ fl oz)	50 g (1¾ oz/⅓ cup)	200 g (7 oz)
DAY 6				
	Second feed 7 am	100 ml (3½ fl oz)	100 g (3½ oz/⅔ cup)	400 g (14 oz)
DAY 7				
	Third feed 7 am	200 ml (7 fl oz)	200 g (7 oz/1⅓ cups)	800 g (1 lb 12 oz)

After the third week, the starter should be strong enough to use in a dough. When you go to make the dough, you need to build up the feeds to make the starter stronger. The day you go to use the starter in a dough, start with 100 g (3½ oz) starter and feed it three times (see chart page 45). It is strongest after the third feed.

If you are making a rye starter adjust the feed amounts above to a ratio of 60% water to 40% organic rye flour. On the day you go to use the rye starter in a dough, start with 100 g (3½ oz) starter and feed it three times, following the chart on page 45 — you will need to adjust the amounts accordingly.

white starter final feeding schedule
week 4

feed time	water	flour	total weight
DOUGH MAKING DAY			
First feed 1 pm	50 ml (1¾ fl oz)	50 g (1¾ oz/⅓ cup)	200 g (7 oz)
Second feed 9 pm	100 ml (3½ fl oz)	100 g (3½ oz/⅔ cup)	400 g (14 oz)
Third feed 6 am	200 ml (7 fl oz)	200 g (7 oz/1⅓ cups)	800 g (1 lb 12 oz)

With this feeding schedule the sourdough or rye dough is best made around 1 pm. There is some give with these times; an hour either side will still be okay. You can alter this schedule to suit the time you want to mix. However, the starter is the most important thing. If it is not ready or not correctly fed, there is no point in mixing a dough.

Once you go to use the starter in a dough, remember to put 100 g (3½ oz) starter aside and continue feeding it for future use. If you are not making bread regularly and you have an established starter, it should survive in the refrigerator being fed once every 2–4 days. You will need to take it out a couple of days before you intend to make a bread dough. Give it sweet loving and three square meals of flour and water on the day the dough is to be made.

It is also possible to freeze a white starter and bring it back with the same love and food as mentioned above. Make sure you freeze the starter in a sterilised bucket when it is at its most active (that is, near the end of the third feed).

tips on feeding a starter

- Always use organic flour and spring water when beginning a starter, as it will increase your chance of success.
- Always use clean plastic buckets when feeding the starter.
- When mixing the flour and water, do not beat it to a paste — mix the flour and water together first, then add the starter and fold it through; a few little lumps of flour are fine as it will make the natural yeasts work a little harder.
- Once you have an active starter the feeding steps become more important as the starter should be bubbly and full of air. You do not want to destroy all that beautiful air, so when you fold through the starter to the feed of flour and water, try to be gentle but thorough.
- Rye flour will ferment more quickly than white flour. You may follow the chart for creating a white starter, but substitute rye flour for white flour during the first week, until the starter is active. After the starter is active you can return to the normal white feeding schedule using white flour. You will basically have a white starter, but one that has had a head start on life.

things to look out for

- If all is going well, your starter should ferment (start bubbling and become frothy) after 1–2 weeks.
- If at any stage your starter has a head of clear liquid on top, this means it is too cold, so place it somewhere warm. It also may mean the starter is hungry, so you need to feed it. Worse still, it may mean your starter has left this world. If you see no activity (bubbling) after two weeks there is something fatally wrong and you will have to start again.
- If the starter has fallen in on itself like a deflated sponge, it is also hungry and may be a little too warm (but active). If this is the case, feed it and move it to a cooler place.
- When the starter is bubbling and frothy and has grown in size, it is happy and well fed and ready to use in your dough.

sourdough

Sourdough is the heart and soul of baking. It's a process that's been around for thousands of years, since the times of the Pharaohs around 1400 BC. As baking has become more sophisticated, with improvements to equipment, machinery and computer technology, sourdough has still survived. In the 1920s, commercial yeast was developed and bread started to be made in large factories, which saw the demise of a lot of local artisan bakeries and sourdough breads. Unfortunately, over time, this industrialised, sliced, bagged and mass-produced bread has lost its nutrition, flavour and connection to the past. Sadly, this 'cottonwool' bread is still the norm in many households today.

But all is not lost. Once people get a taste for sourdough, it's hard to turn back. If you're looking for a wholesome, natural bread that has a low GI (Glycaemic Index), without preservatives or additives then sourdough is the bread for you. Making sourdough bread will take time, but the labour is well worth the effort. You will need to make a starter first, which will act as a rising agent for the bread — it literally starts your sourdough. The only tricky thing about the starter is that it needs to be nurtured and this can sometimes be difficult for those with a busy lifestyle. The solution is simple — try and follow a routine of feeding the starter at the same time each day so it becomes something you do without thinking (see the method on pages 40–5). Feeding the starter is a two-minute process, but the process of developing an active starter can take up to 3–4 weeks. If you think that's a long time, there are starters in bakeries in other countries that are hundreds of years old; at Bourke Street Bakery ours is a mere five years old — just a baby.

405 g (14¼ oz) white starter (see pages 42–5)
765 g (1 lb 11 oz) organic plain flour
400 ml (14 fl oz) water
20 g (¾ oz/2 tablespoons) sea salt

Once you have a starter that is active and dependable, making sourdough is simple. The only hitch is a day-long process that involves a few stages. You will need an oven, flour, water, salt, patience and commitment. To avoid getting up too early, you would look to start mixing the dough in the afternoon and retarding through the night. In theory, you could then roll out of bed and place the loaf in a warm humid place for 1–4 hours and still bake it in time to have fresh bread for lunch. Which is perfect really. Fresh bread should be mandatory for lunch and dinner. For breakfast you are only going to toast it, and this sourdough keeps well for days and is great for toasting.

Once you have mixed the sourdough dough you can use a portion of it to make any of the various derivative doughs on pages 62–95.

sourdough bread

makes 1.5 kg (3lb 5 oz) of dough or 3 loaves

method

To mix the dough by hand, put the starter in a large bowl with the flour and water. Mix together with a large spoon until it comes together to form a dough. Turn out onto a clean work surface and knead into a ball with your hands, for about 10 minutes — the dough does not need to be smooth at this point. Cover with plastic wrap and set aside to rest for 20 minutes. Sprinkle the salt over the dough and knead it for a further 20 minutes or until smooth and elastic.

If you are using an electric mixer, put the starter in the bowl of the mixer with a dough hook attachment. Add the flour and water. Mix on slow speed for 4 minutes, then increase the speed to medium–fast for 3 minutes, or until a rough dough is formed. Cover the bowl and set aside to rest for

20 minutes. Sprinkle the salt over the dough and mix on slow speed for 1 minute. Increase the speed to medium–fast for 6 minutes, or until a smooth elastic dough has formed.

To check the dough has the required structure, roll up a little piece of dough and stretch it out to create a 'window'. If the dough tears at the slightest touch, it is under-mixed and you need to mix it more — what you want is to be able to stretch out the dough to transparency. At this stage the temperature of the dough should be 25°C–27°C (77°F–81°F). If it is below this temperature, leave it to bulk prove in a slightly warmer area. Lightly grease a container with oil spray and sit the dough inside. Cover with plastic wrap and set aside at ambient room temperature (approximately 20°C/68°F) for 1 hour to bulk prove.

To knock back the dough, turn it out onto a lightly floured surface and press out into a rectangle, about 2.5 cm (1 inch) thick. Use your hands to fold one-third back onto itself, then repeat with the remaining third. Turn the dough 90 degrees and fold it over again into thirds. Place the dough back into the oiled container and continue to bulk prove for a further 1 hour.

Use a blunt knife or divider to divide the dough into three even-sized portions, weighing 500 g (1 lb 2 oz) each. Working with one portion of dough at a time, continue to shape the loaves following the instructions for shaping a batard loaf on pages 30–5.

Line three small baskets with a tea towel (dish towel) in each, lightly dust each with flour and place a loaf inside, seam side up. If you are using a cane basket, you don't need the tea towel and can simply dust the basket with flour. Alternatively, you can place the loaves on a baking tray lined with baking paper, seam side down. Place in the refrigerator loosely covered with a plastic bag for 8–12 hours.

Preheat the oven to its highest temperature. Remove the loaves from the refrigerator and let them rest in a warm place (about 25°C/77°F and 80% humidity) for anywhere between 1 and 4 hours depending on the climate. The prove is complete when the loaves have grown in size by two-thirds. If they deflate at the slightest touch they are over-proved and you need to bake them as soon as possible without scoring. If they hold the indent of your finger, they are under-proved and will need more time. If the loaves spring back steadily and quickly when you push lightly into them with a finger then they are ready to bake. Score the loaves (see page 39) and place them in the oven.

Spray the oven with water. Bake for 20 minutes, then turn the loaves or trays around, and bake for a further 10 minutes. Check the base of each loaf with a tap of your finger — if it sounds hollow, it is ready. The bread should take no longer than 40 minutes in total to bake.

ingredients

390 g (13¾ oz) white starter (see pages 42–5)
440 g (15½ oz) organic plain flour
145 g (5¼ oz) organic wholemeal (whole-wheat) flour
145 g (5¼ oz) organic rye flour
360 ml (12½ fl oz) water
20 g (¾ oz/2 tablespoons) sea salt

Back in the olden days, the floor of the flour mill would be swept clean after a hard day's stoneground milling. As the story goes, the remnants of each of the different flours was then collected, bagged and sold as 'millers flour'. This loaf is named millers loaf as it uses a white, wholemeal and rye flours, combining the best of a few worlds. The white flour gives it a lighter characteristic with a more open crumb, while the wholemeal and rye flours add a distinct flavour of the earth and a wholesome healthy aspect. You can use the millers loaf as a base for any of the derivative breads (see pages 62–95).

millers loaf

makes 1.5 kg (3 lb 5 oz) of dough or 3 loaves

method

To mix the millers loaf by hand, put the starter in a large mixing bowl with the plain flour, wholemeal flour and rye flour. Add the water and stir with a large spoon until the mixture comes together to form a dough. Turn out onto a clean work surface and knead into a ball with your hands, for about 10 minutes. Cover with plastic wrap and set aside to rest for 20 minutes. Sprinkle the salt over the dough and knead it for a further 10 minutes. Cover and set aside for 10 minutes. Knead well for a further 5 minutes or until smooth and elastic.

If you are using an electric mixer, put the starter in the bowl of the mixer fitted with a dough hook attachment. Add the combined flours and water. Mix on slow speed for 4 minutes, then increase the speed to medium–fast for 3 minutes. Cover the bowl and set aside to rest for 20 minutes. Sprinkle the salt over the dough and mix on slow speed for 1 minute. Increase the speed to medium–fast for 4–5 minutes, or until a smooth elastic dough forms.

To check the dough has the required structure, roll up a little piece of dough and stretch it out to create a 'window'. If the dough tears at the slightest touch, it is under-mixed and you need to mix it more — what you want is to be able to stretch out the dough to transparency.

Lightly grease a container with oil spray and sit the dough inside. Cover with plastic wrap and set aside at ambient room temperature (approximately 20°C/68°F) for 1 hour to bulk prove.

To knock back the dough, turn it out onto a lightly floured work surface and press out into a rectangle, about 2.5 cm (1 inch) thick. Use your hands to fold one-third back onto itself, then repeat with the remaining third. Turn the dough 90 degrees and fold it over again into thirds. Place the dough back into the oiled container and continue to bulk prove for a further 1 hour.

Use a blunt knife or divider to divide the dough into three even-sized portions, weighing about 500 g (1 lb 2 oz) each. Working with one portion of dough at a time, continue to shape the loaves following the instructions for shaping a round loaf on pages 30–5.

Line three small baskets with a tea towel (dish towel) in each, lightly dust each with flour and place a loaf inside, seam side up. If you are using a cane basket, you don't need the tea towel and can simply dust the basket with flour. Alternatively, you can place the loaves on a baking tray lined with baking paper, seam side down. Place in the refrigerator loosely covered with a plastic bag for 8–12 hours.

Preheat the oven to its highest temperature. Remove the loaves from the refrigerator and let them rest in a humid place, about 25°C (77°F) — this could take anywhere between 1 and 4 hours — until each loaf has grown in size by two-thirds. If the loaves spring back steadily and quickly when you push into them with a finger then they are ready. Score the loaves (see page 39) and place them in the oven.

Spray the oven with water and bake the loaves for 20 minutes, then turn the loaves or trays around, and bake for a further 10 minutes, watching carefully to make sure that the loaves do not burn. Check the base of each loaf with a tap of your finger — if it sounds hollow, it is ready. Baking should take no longer than 40 minutes in total.

ingredients

310 g (11 oz) white starter (see pages 42–5)
810 g (1 lb 12½ oz) organic white spelt flour
360 ml (12½ fl oz) water
15 g (½ oz/1½ tablespoons) sea salt

Spelt is a member of the wheat family but pre-dates wheat;
many moons ago it was common in the fields of Europe.
The main difference between the two is that the spelt kernel
has a tough outer hull that does not come off when threshed.
The spelt kernel is sent away to be threshed through
a special machine, which is why it is unloved by farmers
and consequently more expensive to purchase.

People often think that spelt loaves are gluten-free but this
is not the case. The spelt sourdough contains a fair amount
of gluten, although the gluten that it does contain is easier to
digest than standard wheat flour. If you are seriously affected
by gluten, a 100 per cent rye loaf is a much better option.
Spelt is also low on the glycaemic index and a good option for
diabetics. This loaf has a lovely caramel flavour and texture and
if you close your eyes really tight you can almost taste the past.

spelt sourdough
makes 1.5 kg (3 lb 5 oz) of dough or 3 loaves

method

To mix the spelt sourdough by hand, put the starter in a large mixing bowl
with the spelt flour and water. Mix together with a large spoon until the
mixture comes together to form a dough. Turn out onto a clean work surface
and knead into a ball for about 10 minutes. Cover with plastic wrap and set
aside to rest for 20 minutes. Sprinkle the salt over the dough and knead it
for a further 10 minutes. Cover and set aside for 10 minutes. Knead well for
a further 5 minutes, or until smooth and elastic.

If you are using an electric mixer, put the starter in the bowl of the mixer
fitted with the dough hook attachment. Add the spelt flour and water. Mix
on slow speed for 4 minutes, then increase the speed to medium–fast for

3 minutes. Cover the bowl and set aside to rest for 20 minutes. Sprinkle the salt over the dough and mix on slow speed for 1 minute. Increase the speed to medium–fast for 6 minutes, or until smooth and elastic.

To check the dough has the required structure, roll up a little piece of dough and stretch it out to create a 'window'. If the dough tears at the slightest touch, it is under-mixed and you need to mix it more — what you want is to be able to stretch out the dough to transparency.

Lightly grease a container with oil spray and sit the dough inside. Cover with plastic wrap and set aside at ambient room temperature (approximately 20°C/68°F) for 1 hour to bulk prove.

To knock back the dough, turn it out onto a lightly floured work surface and press out into a rectangle, about 2.5 cm (1 inch) thick. Use your hands to fold one-third back onto itself, then repeat with the remaining third. Turn the dough 90 degrees and fold it over again into thirds. Place the dough back into the oiled container and continue to bulk prove for a further 1 hour.

Use a blunt knife or divider to divide the dough into three even-sized portions, weighing about 500 g (1 lb 2 oz) each. Working with one portion of dough at a time, continue to shape the loaves following the instructions for shaping a batard loaf on pages 30–5.

Line three small baskets with a tea towel (dish towel) in each, lightly dust each with flour and place a loaf inside, seam side up. If you are using a traditional cane basket, you don't need the tea towel and can simply dust the basket with flour. Alternatively, you can place the loaves on a baking tray lined with baking paper, seam side down. Place in the refrigerator loosely covered with a plastic bag for 8–12 hours.

Preheat the oven to its highest temperature. Remove the loaves from the refrigerator and let them rest in a humid place, about 25°C (77°F) — this could take anywhere between 1 and 4 hours — until each loaf has grown in size by two-thirds. If the loaves push back steadily and quickly when you push lightly into them with a finger then they are ready. Score the loaves (see page 39) and place them in the oven.

Spray the oven with water and bake the loaves for 20 minutes, then turn the loaves or trays around, and bake for a further 10 minutes, watching carefully to make sure that the loaves do not burn. Check the base of each loaf with a tap of your finger — if it sounds hollow, it is ready. Baking should take no longer than 40 minutes in total.

100% rye bread

makes 2.4 kg (5 lb 4 oz) of dough or 3 loaves

This loaf relies on you having a really good rye starter. Rye flour does not have the high gluten content of wheat grain and as a result has little capacity to stretch, trap and hold air bubbles and create a structure that will prove and rise.

A naturally leavened loaf of 100 per cent rye will be quite dense by nature. Rye bread will stay fresh longer than other breads. There are two reasons rye bread takes longer to stale: it is hydroscopic, so it absorbs moisture from the air and it is almost gluten-free. All in all, rye bread is better for you, better for your stomach, better for your bowel, better for your soul, but not great for a burger.

Rye loaves need help when proving and baking, so a bread tin is used to provide the much-needed scaffolding as it slowly rises. When in the oven, a rye loaf has a tendency to dry out, so a tin also helps to retain some of the moisture.

method

To mix the rye dough by hand, put the starter in a large mixing bowl with the flour, salt, molasses and water. Mix together with a large spoon until the mixture comes together to form a dough, about 15 minutes — it may be a bit sticky to begin with but persevere. Turn out onto a clean work surface and knead into a ball with your hands for about 10 minutes, or until smooth but slightly sticky.

If you are using an electric mixer, put the starter in the bowl of the mixer with the dough hook attachment. Add the flour, salt, molasses and water. Mix on slow speed for 8 minutes, then increase the speed to high for 1 minute, or until combined. As rye flour has a minuscule gluten percentage, there is no need to mix it at high speed for long as there is nothing much to stretch.

Lightly grease a container with oil spray and sit the dough inside. Cover with plastic wrap and set aside at ambient room temperature (approximately 20°C/68°F) for 1 hour to bulk prove.

To knock back the dough, turn it out onto a lightly floured surface and press out into a rectangle, about 2.5 cm (1 inch) thick. Use your hands to fold one-third back onto itself, then repeat with the remaining third. Turn the dough 90 degrees and fold it over again into thirds. Place the dough back into the oiled container and continue to prove for a further 30 minutes.

Use a blunt knife or divider to divide the dough into three even-sized portions, weighing 800 g (1 lb 12 oz) each. Working with one portion of dough at a time, surround the dough with your cupped hands, always keeping your hands in contact with the dough. In an anti-clockwise motion, start rolling the dough to create a tight ball with a smooth surface. Set aside on a lightly floured surface for 20 minutes, covered with plastic wrap.

Lightly grease three 15 x 9 cm (6 x 3½ inch) loaf (bar) tins, about 10 cm (4 inches) deep. Working with one ball of dough at a time, stretch each dough portion out to double its width. Fold a third into itself towards the middle, then fold in the other third to overlap. Then, as if you are making a paper aeroplane, fold it in to create the nose cone at the end furthest from the edge of the bench. Press this down to prevent any large air pockets forming.

Bring the dough into the shape that will be placed into the tin. With your fingers tensed, press down onto the nose cone and fold inwards keeping the action tight — this is called crimping. Use small movements with your fingers, folding over the dough and pressing down as you work to create tension and form. Crimp with your fingers until you reach halfway into the dough, then with the ball of your dominant hand press down against the seam closing

it into the dough. Continue this motion with both hands, folding the dough over in tight movements, each time closing the seam. Check to see that the seam is straight and closed; if not, pinch the seam to close it. Place the dough in the tins and cover loosely with plastic wrap.

Proving the rye is best done at ambient room temperature (20°C/68°F) for 6–12 hours. It does not benefit from a long slow cold prove as the starter will just not be strong enough. The loaf should grow by one-third. There will be no spring-back when you touch the loaf.

Preheat the oven to 200°C (400°F/Gas 6). Spray the oven with water and reduce the temperature to 150°C (300°F/Gas 2). Bake for 25 minutes, then turn the loaves or trays around, and bake for a further 15 minutes. Check the base of each loaf with a tap of your finger — it should make a dull hollow sound when it is ready. Baking should take no longer than 50 minutes in total. If you cut into a baked loaf and it has a gooey line at its base, you have taken it out of the oven a little too early.

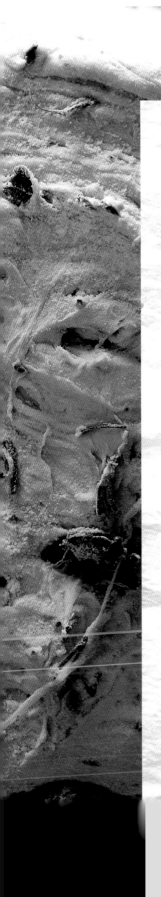

derivative breads

Once you have a basic white sourdough, millers sourdough or spelt sourdough you can create other variations from it. Adding nuts, fruit, spices or vegetables to a plain loaf can produce a variety of results. Rye starter is a recurring theme of derivative doughs and will add a nutty, earthy flavour that we like at Bourke Street. The rye starter also helps to incorporate the additional ingredients that you are adding, acting as a kind of lubricant.

With the recipes in this section you will need about 715–890 g (1 lb 9 oz– 1 lb 16 oz) of sourdough. A standard recipe of white sourdough allows you to make 1.5 kg (3 lb 5 oz) of dough, so you will have about 610–785 g (1 lb 5 oz– 1 lb 12 oz) of white sourdough left over. You can either make two varieties of the derivative doughs, or use the leftover to bake a plain white sourdough. If you bake a larger loaf, follow the same baking directions as for white sourdough and bake it for a little longer, about 45 minutes for a 785 g (1 lb 12 oz) loaf.

You need to be careful when mixing the extra ingredients into the derivative doughs, making sure that you don't break down the dough too much. Any fast mixing with other ingredients may rip apart the already developed gluten strands. All you are really trying to do is fold the new ingredients through the dough. With a mixer, it should take no longer than a few minutes on slow speed. You will need to give it a helping hand by stopping the mixer a few times to push the dough around the bowl. By hand, it should take a little longer. This method is the same no matter what you are folding through.

Baking times for the derivative doughs may vary depending on the additional ingredients. They will not be widely different from a basic sourdough loaf, however, if you add an ingredient with a lot of natural sugar, such as the fruit soak, you need to watch the loaf carefully when it approaches the end of its baking time as the outside is more likely to burn faster.

ingredients

fruit soak (makes 220g/7³⁄₄ oz)

50 g (1³⁄₄ oz/¹⁄₃ cup) currants

150 g (5¹⁄₂ oz/1¹⁄₄ cups) raisins

140 ml (4³⁄₄ fl oz) water

720 g (1 lb 9¹⁄₂ oz) sourdough dough (see pages 50–1)

70 g (2¹⁄₂ oz/¹⁄₂ cup) whole roasted and peeled hazelnuts

85 g (3 oz) rye starter (see pages 43–5)

Also known as 'hazel razel', this popular bread was one of those doughs that started life as yeasted dough and then morphed into a sourdough. This is a lovely fruit loaf strewn with whole hazelnuts, soaked currants and raisins. When toasted, the hazelnuts crisp up and become even more aromatic. It tastes particularly good with fresh ricotta or jam, and our customers tell us it also makes a scrumptious bread and butter pudding.

hazelnut and raisin loaf

makes 2 loaves

method

To make the fruit soak, put the currants and raisins in a bowl and pour over the water. Cover with plastic wrap and soak the fruit overnight. Drain the fruit, discarding the water, and set aside until needed.

Follow the instructions for mixing a sourdough loaf on pages 50–1 until you can create a window. Measure 125 g (4¹⁄₂ oz) of the fruit soak and combine with the hazelnuts and rye starter. Lightly mix through the dough until just combined. You can do this by hand by lightly folding the ingredients through the dough or simply add it to the bowl of an electric mixer and mix for 2–3 minutes on slow speed — you will need to give it a helping hand by stopping the mixer a few times to push the dough around the bowl. Lightly grease a container with oil spray and sit the dough inside. Cover with plastic wrap and set aside at ambient room temperature (approximately 20°C/68°F) for 1 hour to bulk prove.

To knock back the dough, turn it out onto a lightly floured work surface and press out into a rectangle, about 2.5 cm (1 inch) thick. Use your hands to fold one-third back onto itself, then repeat with the remaining third. Turn the dough 90 degrees and fold it over again into thirds. Place the dough back into the oiled container and continue to bulk prove for a further 1 hour.

Use a blunt knife or divider to divide the dough into two even-sized portions, weighing about 500 g (1 lb 2 oz) each. Working with one portion of dough at a time, continue to shape the loaves following the instructions for shaping a round loaf on pages 30–5.

Line two small baskets with a tea towel (dish towel) in each, lightly dust both with flour and place the dough inside, seam side up, so that when you go to turn the loaves out onto trays it is with the seam down onto the tray. If you are using a cane basket, you don't need the tea towel and can simply dust the basket with flour. Alternatively, you can place the loaves on a baking tray lined with baking paper, seam side down. Place in the refrigerator loosely covered with a plastic bag for 8–12 hours.

Preheat the oven to its highest temperature. Remove the loaves from the refrigerator and let them rest, covered, in a humid place (25°C/77°F) — this could take anywhere between 1 and 4 hours — until each loaf has grown in size by two-thirds. If the loaves push back steadily and quickly when you push lightly into them with a finger then they are ready to bake. Score the loaves (see page 39) and place in the oven.

Spray the oven with water and reduce the temperature to 220°C (425°F/Gas 7). Bake the loaves for 20 minutes, then turn the loaves or trays around and bake for a further 10 minutes, watching carefully to make sure that the loaves do not burn. Check the base of each loaf with a tap of your finger — if it sounds hollow, it is ready. Baking should take no longer than 40 minutes in total.

note

If you need to adjust the weight of the fruit soak recipe, work on the ratio of one-third currants to two-thirds raisins — you will still need to weigh the fruit accurately before adding to a loaf. Any left-over fruit soak can be stored in an airtight container for up to 1 month in the refrigerator — but you should have eaten it by then, scattered over your cereal.

ingredients

725 g (1 lb 9½ oz) sourdough dough (see pages 50–1)

10g (¼ oz) barberries

40 g (1½ oz) fruit soak (see page 64)

145 g (5 ¼ oz/¾ cup) dried figs, cut into sixths

85 g (3 oz) rye starter (see pages 43–5)

This loaf does everything a fruit loaf should do. Great for toast in the morning, terrific as a cheese and wine accompaniment and like the hazelnut and raisin loaf on pages 64–5 it is very yummy as the bread component of a bread and butter pudding. A barberry is a sour berry from Iran similar to a cranberry and packed full of sour-sweet flavours. Barberries are available from Middle Eastern food stores and specialist delicatessens.

fig and barberry loaf makes 2 loaves

method

To make the fig and barberry loaf, follow the instructions for mixing sourdough on pages 50–1 until you can create a window. Lightly mix in the combined barberries, fruit soak, figs and rye starter. You can do this by hand by lightly folding the ingredients through the dough or simply add it to the bowl of an electric mixer and mix for 2–3 minutes on slow speed — you will need to give it a helping hand by stopping the mixer a few times to push the dough around the bowl. Lightly grease a container with oil spray and sit the dough inside. Cover with plastic wrap and set aside at ambient room temperature (approximately 20°C/68°F) for 1 hour to bulk prove.

To knock back the dough, turn it out onto a lightly floured work surface and press out into a rectangle, about 2.5 cm (1 inch) thick. Use your hands to fold one-third back onto itself, then repeat with the remaining third. Turn the dough 90 degrees and fold it over again into thirds. Place the dough back into the oiled container and continue to bulk prove for a further 1 hour.

Use a blunt knife or divider to divide the dough into two even-sized portions, about 500 g (1 lb 2 oz). Working with one portion of dough at a time, continue to shape the loaves following the instructions for shaping a batard loaf on pages 30–5.

Line two small baskets with a tea towel (dish towel) in each, lightly dust both with flour and place a loaf inside each, seam side up. If you are using a cane basket, you don't need the tea towel and can simply dust the basket with flour. Alternatively, you can place the loaves on a baking tray lined with baking paper, seam side down. Place in the refrigerator loosely covered with a plastic bag for 8–12 hours.

Preheat the oven to its highest temperature. Remove the covered loaves from the refrigerator and let them rest in a humid place (25°C/77°F) — this could take anywhere between 1 and 4 hours — until each loaf has grown in size by two-thirds. If the loaves push back steadily and quickly when you push lightly into them with a finger then they are ready. Score the loaves (see page 39) and place in the oven.

Spray the oven with water and reduce the temperature to 220°C (425°F/Gas 7). Bake the loaves for 20 minutes, then turn the loaves or trays around, and bake for a further 10 minutes, watching carefully to make sure that the loaves do not burn. Check the base of each loaf with a tap of your finger — if it sounds hollow, it is ready. Baking should take no longer than 40 minutes in total.

The fig and barberry loaf is the most popular fruit loaf at Bourke Street Bakery, with figs from Turkey, barberries from Iran, flour from Gunnedah, salt from the Murray River, raisins from California, currants from Victoria and water from Warragamba. This loaf deserves its status — it is a perfectly natural mix of sweet and sour. The crumbling figs melt in your mouth and taste so good that it is tempting to pull them off the loaf and eat them even before the bread knife comes out.

ingredients

25 g (1 oz) rye grain or quinoa

70 ml (2¼ fl oz) water

20 g (¾ oz/2 tablespoons) sunflower seeds

865 g (1 lb 14½ oz) sourdough dough (see pages 50–1)

5 g (⅛ oz/2½ teaspoons) caraway seeds

½ teaspoon cumin seeds

90 g (3¼ oz) rye starter (see pages 43–5)

This rye and caraway loaf is a favourite at Bourke Street Bakery. We tried to take this loaf off the menu once and lived to regret it. A backlash ensued — not quite people marching in the streets, but we did receive a dozen angry emails. Rightly so.

This loaf provides a meal in a slice, with great flavour and texture. The cumin seeds came late to the recipe. Like many great discoveries, it happened by accident when an apprentice, not knowing the difference between cumin and caraway seeds, topped up the caraway bucket with cumin seeds — voila! You will need to soak the rye grain in water for two days before you make this loaf.

rye and caraway loaf

makes 2 loaves

method

Put the rye grain in a bowl and pour over the water. Cover with plastic wrap and set aside to soak for 2 days. Drain well and set aside until needed.

To toast the sunflower seeds, cool them on a baking tray in a preheated 180°C (350°C/Gas 4) oven for about 8 minutes, or until lightly toasted. Set aside and allow to cool completely before adding to the dough.

To make the rye and caraway loaf, follow the instructions for mixing sourdough on pages 50–1 until you can create a window. Lightly mix in the rye grain, combined seeds and rye starter. You can do this by hand by lightly folding the ingredients through the dough until just combined, or simply add it to the bowl of an electric mixer and mix for 2–3 minutes on slow speed — you will need to give it a helping hand by stopping the mixer a few times to push the dough around the bowl. Lightly grease a container with oil spray and sit the dough inside. Cover with plastic wrap and set aside at ambient room temperature (approximately 20°C/68°F) for 1 hour to bulk prove.

To knock back the dough, turn it out onto a lightly floured work surface and press out into a rectangle, about 2.5 cm (1 inch) thick. Use your hands to fold one-third back onto itself, then repeat with the remaining third. Turn the dough 90 degrees and fold it over again into thirds. Place the dough back into the oiled container and continue to bulk prove for a further 1 hour.

Use a blunt knife or divider to divide the dough into two even-sized portions, about 500 g (1 lb 2 oz) each. Working with one portion of dough at a time, continue to shape the loaves following the instructions for shaping a round loaf on pages 30–5.

Line two small baskets with a tea towel (dish towel) in each, lightly dust both with flour and place a loaf inside each, seam side up. If you are using a traditional cane basket, you don't need the tea towel and can simply dust the basket with flour. Alternatively, you can place the loaves on a baking tray lined with baking paper, seam side down. Place in the refrigerator loosely covered with a plastic bag for 8–12 hours.

Preheat the oven to its highest temperature. Remove the loaves from the refrigerator and let them rest in a humid place (25°C/77°F) — this could take anywhere between 1 and 4 hours — until each loaf has grown in size by two-thirds. If the loaves push back steadily and quickly when you push lightly into them with a finger then they are ready. Score the loaves (see page 39) and place in the oven.

Spray the oven with water and bake the loaves for 20 minutes, then turn the loaves or trays around, and bake for a further 10 minutes, watching carefully to make sure that the loaves do not burn. Check the base of each loaf with a tap of your finger — if it sounds hollow, it is ready. Baking should take no longer than 40 minutes in total.

ingredients
775 g (1 lb 11¼ oz) sourdough dough (see pages 50–1)
1 teaspoon ground cinnamon
½ teaspoon ground allspice
¾ teaspoon ground nutmeg
½ teaspoon ground cloves
220 g (7¾ oz) fruit soak (see page 64)

At Bourke Street Bakery we mix together allspice, nutmeg, cloves, cinnamon and fruit soak through the basic sourdough to create this loaf. In our first year of trading we sold these loaves as a hot cross bun substitute (as we did not have a bun divider, it would have been extremely time-consuming to try and make a serious quantity of hot cross buns). This was justified by the un-researched fact that when the hot cross bun evolved they would have been sourdough-based.

spiced fruit sourdough

makes 2 loaves

method
To make the spiced fruit sourdough, follow the instructions for mixing sourdough on pages 50–1 until you can create a window. Lightly mix in the combined spices and fruit soak. You can do this by hand by lightly folding the ingredients through the dough until just combined, or simply add it to the bowl of an electric mixer and mix for 2–3 minutes on slow speed — you will need to give it a helping hand by stopping the mixer a few times to push the dough around the bowl. Lightly grease a container with oil spray and sit the dough inside. Cover with plastic wrap and set aside at ambient room temperature (approximately 20°C/68°F) for 1 hour to bulk prove.

To knock back the dough, turn it out onto a lightly floured surface and press out into a rectangle, about 2.5 cm (1 inch) thick. Use your hands to fold one third back onto itself, then repeat with the remaining third. Turn the dough 90 degrees and fold it over again into thirds. Place the dough back into the oiled container and continue to bulk prove for a further 1 hour.

Use a blunt knife or divider to divide the dough into two even-sized portions, about 500 g (1 lb 2 oz) each. Working with one portion of dough at a time, continue to shape the loaves following the instructions for shaping a round loaf on pages 30–5.

Line two small baskets with a tea towel (dish towel) in each, lightly dust both with flour and place a loaf inside each, seam side up. If you are using a traditional cane basket, you don't need the tea towel and can simply dust the basket with flour. Alternatively, you can place the loaves on a baking tray lined with baking paper, seam side down. Place in the refrigerator loosely covered with a plastic bag for 8–12 hours.

Preheat the oven to its highest temperature. Remove the loaves from the refrigerator and let them rest in a humid place (25°C/77°F) — this could take anywhere between 1 and 4 hours — until each loaf has grown in size by two-thirds. If the loaves push back steadily and quickly when you push lightly into them with a finger then they are ready. Score the loaves (see page 39) and place in the oven.

Spray the oven with water and reduce the temperature to 220°C (425°F/Gas 7). Bake the loaves for 20 minutes, then turn the loaves or trays around, and bake for a further 10 minutes, watching carefully to make sure that the loaves do not burn. Check the base of each loaf with a tap of your finger — if it sounds hollow, it is ready. Baking should take no longer than 40 minutes in total.

ingredients

30 g (1 oz) dried organic soy beans
300 ml (10½ fl oz) water
890 g (1 lb 16 oz) sourdough dough (see pages 50–1)
20 g (¾ oz/1½ tablespoons) linseeds (flax seeds)
30 g (1 oz/⅓ cup) soy flour

A great healthy alternative for a sandwich, this is the loaf we use for the vegetarian sandwiches we make at Bourke Street Bakery. It has a lovely crunchy texture that makes you feel like you are living longer. You will need to soak the soy beans the day before you wish to make this loaf.

soy bean and linseed loaf

makes 2 loaves

method

Put the soy beans and water in a bowl. Cover with plastic wrap and set aside overnight to soak. Drain the beans and set aside until needed.

To make the soy bean and linseed loaf, follow the instructions for mixing sourdough on pages 50–1 until you can create a window. Slowly sprinkle the linseeds over the sourdough. Lightly mix in the soy beans and soy flour. You can do this by hand by lightly folding the ingredients through the dough until just combined, or simply add it to the bowl of an electric mixer and mix for 2–3 minutes on slow speed. Lightly grease a container with oil spray and sit the dough inside. Cover with plastic wrap and set aside at ambient room temperature (approximately 20°C/68°F) for 1 hour to bulk prove.

To knock back the dough, turn it out onto a lightly floured work surface and press out into a rectangle, about 2.5 cm (1 inch) thick. Use your hands to fold one-third back onto itself, then repeat with the remaining third. Turn the dough 90 degrees and fold it over again into thirds. Place the dough back into the oiled container and continue to bulk prove for a further 1 hour.

Use a blunt knife or divider to divide the dough into two even-sized portions, about 500 g (1 lb 2 oz) each. Working with one portion of dough at a time, continue to shape the loaves following the instructions for shaping a batard loaf on pages 30–5.

Line two small baskets with a tea towel (dish towel) in each, lightly dust both with flour and place a loaf inside each, seam side up. If you are using a traditional cane basket, you don't need the tea towel and can simply dust the basket with flour. Alternatively, you can place the loaves on a baking tray lined with baking paper, seam side down. Place in the refrigerator loosely covered with a plastic bag for 8–12 hours.

Preheat the oven to its highest temperature. Remove the covered loaves from the refrigerator and let them rest in a humid place (25°C/77°F) — this could take anywhere between 1 and 4 hours — until each loaf has grown in size by two-thirds. If the loaves push back steadily and quickly when you push lightly into them with a finger then they are ready. Score the loaves (see page 39) and place in the oven.

Spray the oven with water and bake the loaves for 20 minutes, then turn the loaves or trays around, and bake for a further 10 minutes, watching carefully to make sure that the loaves do not burn. Check the base of each loaf with a tap of your finger — if it sounds hollow, it is ready. Baking should take no longer than 40 minutes in total.

ingredients

70 g (2½ oz) walnuts

725 g (1 lb 9½ oz) sourdough dough (see pages 50–1)

125 g (4½ oz) fruit soak (see page 64)

90 g (3¼ oz) rye starter (see pages 43–5)

The walnut and currant loaf is best paired with some good cheese, where it can achieve true greatness. Ricotta and quince are also close friends. Releasing the natural oils by roasting the walnuts makes a big difference to this loaf.

walnut and currant loaf

makes 2 loaves

method

To roast the walnuts, cook them on a baking tray in a preheated 180°C (350°F/Gas 4) oven for about 7 minutes, or until golden. Allow to cool completely before adding to the dough.

To make the walnut and currant loaf, follow the instructions for mixing sourdough on pages 50–1 until you can create a window. Lightly mix in the combined walnuts, fruit soak and rye starter. You can do this by hand by lightly folding the ingredients through the dough until just combined, or simply add it to the bowl of an electric mixer and mix for 2–3 minutes on slow speed. Lightly grease a container with oil spray and sit the dough inside. Cover with plastic wrap and set aside at ambient room temperature (approximately 20°C/68°F) for 1 hour to bulk prove.

To knock back the dough, turn it out onto a lightly floured work surface and press out into a rectangle, about 2.5 cm (1 inch) thick. Use your hands to fold one-third back onto itself, then repeat with the remaining third. Turn the dough 90 degrees and fold it over again into thirds. Place the dough back into the oiled container and continue to bulk prove for a further 1 hour.

Use a blunt knife or divider to divide the dough into two even-sized portions, about 500 g (1 lb 2 oz) each. Working with one portion of dough at a time, continue to shape the loaves following the instructions for shaping a round loaf on pages 30–5.

Line two small baskets with a tea towel (dish towel) in each, lightly dust both with flour and place a loaf inside each, seam side up. If you are using a traditional cane basket, you don't need the tea towel and can simply dust the basket with flour. Alternatively, you can place the loaves on a baking tray lined with baking paper, seam side down. Place in the refrigerator loosely covered with a plastic bag for 8–12 hours.

Preheat the oven to its highest temperature. Remove the loaves from the refrigerator and let them rest in a humid place (25°C/77°F) — this could take anywhere between 1 and 4 hours — until each loaf has grown in size by two-thirds. If the loaves push back steadily and quickly when you push lightly into them with a finger then they are ready. Score the loaves (see page 39) and place in the oven.

Spray the oven with water and reduce the temperature to 220°C (425°F/Gas 7). Bake the loaves for 20 minutes, then turn the loaves or trays around, and bake for a further 10 minutes, watching carefully to make sure that the loaves do not burn. Check the base of each loaf with a tap of your finger — if it sounds hollow, it is ready. Baking should take no longer than 40 minutes in total.

70 g (2½ oz) organic rolled (porridge) oats

40 ml (1¼ fl oz) water

715 g (1 lb 9 oz) sourdough dough (see pages 50–1)

185 g (6½ oz) apples, peeled, cored and cut into 2–3 cm (¾–1¼ inch) pieces

A solid healthy option for breakfast with cottage cheese or ricotta, the apple and oat loaf is also good for a cheese plate as it has quite a subdued flavour and lets the cheese take all the tastebud glory. The oats gives this loaf a porridge-like texture, which becomes quite crumbly when toasted. This loaf generally takes a little longer to prove and a little longer to bake than other loaves, as the internal crumb of the loaf is held down by the oats. If you wish, you can play around with the ratio of oats to dough in this loaf and change its texture. Reducing the quantity of oats will mean it will not be as dense and can be cooked for a little less time.

apple and oat loaf

makes 2 loaves

method

Put the rolled oats in a bowl and pour over the water. Leave to soak for 5 minutes, cover with plastic wrap and set aside until needed.

To make the apple and oat loaf, follow the instructions for mixing sourdough on pages 50–1 until you can create a window. Lightly mix in the combined apple and soaked oats. You can do this by hand by lightly folding the ingredients through the dough until just combined, or simply add it to the bowl of an electric mixer and mix for 2–3 minutes on slow speed — you will need to give it a helping hand by stopping the mixer a few times to push the dough around the bowl. Lightly grease a container with oil spray and sit the dough inside. Cover with plastic wrap and set aside at ambient room temperature (approximately 20°C/68°F) for 1 hour to bulk prove.

To knock back the dough, turn it out onto a lightly floured work surface and press out into a rectangle, about 2.5 cm (1 inch) thick. Use your hands to fold one-third back onto itself, then repeat with the remaining third. Turn the dough 90 degrees and fold it over again into thirds. Place the dough back into the oiled container and continue to bulk prove for a further 1 hour.

Use a blunt knife or divider to divide the dough into two even-sized portions, about 500 g (1 lb 2 oz) each. Working with one portion of dough at a time, continue to shape the loaves following the instructions for shaping a round loaf on pages 30–5.

Line two small baskets with a tea towel (dish towel) in each, lightly dust both with flour and place a loaf inside each, seam side up. If you are using a traditional cane basket, you don't need the tea towel and can simply dust the basket with flour. Alternatively, you can place the loaves on a baking tray lined with baking paper, seam side down. Place in the refrigerator loosely covered with a plastic bag for 8–12 hours.

Preheat the oven to its highest temperature. Remove the covered loaves from the refrigerator and let them rest in a humid place (25°C/77°F) — this could take anywhere between 1 and 4 hours — until each loaf has grown in size by two-thirds. If the loaves push back steadily and quickly when you push lightly into them with a finger then they are ready. Score the loaves (see page 39) and place them in the oven.

Spray the oven with water and reduce the temperature to 220°C (425°F/ Gas 7). Bake the loaves for 25 minutes, then turn the loaves or trays around, and bake for a further 10 minutes, watching carefully to make sure that the loaves do not burn. Check the base of each loaf with a tap of your finger — the mysterious hollow sound is harder to achieve with this loaf as the oats change the loaf's density — you can hear it but it will be a bit duller than usual. Baking should take no longer than 40 minutes in total.

ingredients

775 g (1 lb 11¼ oz) sourdough dough (see pages 50–1)

5 g (⅛ oz/2½ teaspoons) whole fennel seeds

175 g (6 oz) fruit soak (see page 64)

55 g (2 oz) rye starter (see pages 43–5)

Fennel seed is a much-loved seed at Bourke Street Bakery. We are not the only ones who love it, as it features prominently in Italian, Indian and Middle Eastern cooking. The fennel seed also has a minor role in Chinese, Malaysian and German cookery. It has an intense anise flavour that is unmistakable.

anise fruit sourdough

makes 2 loaves

method

To make the anise fruit sourdough, follow the instructions for mixing sourdough on pages 50–1 until you can create a window. Lightly mix in the fennel seeds, fruit soak and rye starter. You can do this by hand by lightly folding the ingredients through the dough until just combined, or simply add it to the bowl of an electric mixer and mix for 2–3 minutes on slow speed — you will need to give it a helping hand by stopping the mixer a few times to push the dough around the bowl. Lightly grease a container with oil spray and sit the dough inside. Cover with plastic wrap and set aside at ambient room temperature (approximately 20°C/68°F) for 1 hour to bulk prove.

To knock back the dough, turn it out onto a lightly floured work surface and press out into a rectangle, about 2.5 cm (1 inch) thick. Use your hands to fold one-third back onto itself, then repeat with the remaining third. Turn the dough 90 degrees and fold it over again into thirds. Place the dough back into the oiled container and continue to bulk prove for a further 1 hour.

Use a blunt knife or divider to divide the dough into two even-sized portions, about 500 g (1 lb 2 oz) each. Working with one portion of dough at a time, continue to shape the loaves following the instructions for shaping a round loaf on pages 30–5.

Line two small baskets with a tea towel (dish towel) in each, lightly dust both with flour and place a loaf inside each, seam side up. If you are using a traditional cane basket, you don't need the tea towel and can simply dust the basket with flour. Alternatively, you can place the loaves on a baking tray lined with baking paper, seam side down. Place in the refrigerator loosely covered with a plastic bag for 8–12 hours.

Preheat the oven to its highest temperature. Remove the loaves from the refrigerator and let them rest in a humid place (25°C/77°F) — this could take anywhere between 1 and 4 hours — until each loaf has grown in size by two-thirds. If the loaves push back steadily and quickly when you push lightly into them with a finger then they are ready. Score the loaves (see page 39) and place them in the oven.

Spray the oven with water and reduce the temperature to 220°C (425°F/Gas 7). Bake the loaves for 20 minutes, then turn the loaves or trays around, and bake for a further 10 minutes, watching carefully to make sure that the loaves do not burn. Check the base of each loaf with a tap of your finger — if it sounds hollow, it is ready. Baking should take no longer than 40 minutes in total.

ingredients

125 g (4½ oz) desiree potatoes, cut into
3 cm (1¼ inch) cubes

30 ml (1 fl oz/1½ tablespoons) olive oil

a pinch of salt

a pinch of freshly ground black pepper

830 g (1 lb 13¼ oz) sourdough dough
(see pages 50–1)

6 rosemary sprigs, leaves picked

20 g (¾ oz/2 tablespoons) soy flour

5 g (⅛ oz/2 teaspoons) nigella seeds

This is another dough that went through its adolescence with yeast, then grew up into an honest sourdough (see page 108 for the recipe for potato bread junior). We use desiree potatoes as they are consistently good all year round, but you can use any potato really. The potatoes are first tossed in olive oil, then seasoned and roasted in a hot oven to partially cook them before adding to the dough. Nigella seeds are also called kalonji at the Indian grocer and are often mistakenly called black or cumin seeds.

mr potato bread

makes 2 loaves

method

Preheat the oven to 220°C (425°F/Gas 7). Put the potato cubes in a baking tray and pour over 3 teaspoons of the olive oil. Season with salt and freshly ground black pepper and bake in the oven for 15 minutes, or until a knife can nearly pierce through the potato easily. Allow to cool. The potatoes only need to be half-cooked at this stage as they will continue cooking when the loaf is baked. If the potatoes are overcooked they will disintegrate when you go to fold them through the dough. What you want is to be able to slice a piece of potato bread and see nice chunks of potato, which will signify that this is a handmade loaf.

To make the potato bread, follow the instructions for mixing sourdough on pages 50–1 until you can create a window. Use your hands to lightly

fold the potato, rosemary, soy flour, nigella seeds and remaining oil into the dough until just combined. You can do this by hand by lightly folding the ingredients through the dough until just combined, or simply add it to the bowl of an electric mixer and mix for 2–3 minutes on very slow speed — you will need to give it a helping hand by stopping the mixer a few times to push the dough around the bowl and be careful not to break up the potato too much. Lightly grease a container with oil spray and sit the dough inside. Cover with plastic wrap and set aside at ambient room temperature (approximately 20°C/68°F) for 1 hour to bulk prove.

To knock back the dough, turn it out onto a lightly floured work surface and press out into a rectangle, about 2.5 cm (1 inch) thick. Use your hands to fold one-third back onto itself, then repeat with the remaining third. Turn the dough 90 degrees and fold it over again into thirds. Place the dough back into the oiled container and continue to bulk prove for a further 1 hour.

Use a blunt knife or divider to divide the dough into two even-sized portions, about 500 g (1 lb 2 oz) each. Working with one portion of dough at a time, continue to shape the loaves following the instructions for shaping a round loaf on pages 30–5.

Line two small baskets with a tea towel (dish towel) in each, lightly dust both with flour and place a loaf inside each, seam side up. If you are using a traditional cane basket, you don't need the tea towel and can simply dust the basket with flour. Alternatively, you can place the loaves on a baking tray lined with baking paper, seam side down. Place in the refrigerator loosely covered with a plastic bag for 8–12 hours.

Preheat the oven to its highest temperature. Remove the loaves from the refrigerator and let them rest in a humid place (25°C/77°F) — this could take anywhere between 1 and 4 hours — until each loaf has grown in size by two-thirds. If the loaves push back steadily and quickly when you push lightly into them with a finger then they are ready. Score the loaves if you like (see page 39) and place them in the oven.

Spray the oven with water and reduce the temperature to 220°C (425°F/Gas 7). Bake the loaves for 20 minutes, then turn the loaves or trays around, and bake for a further 10 minutes, watching carefully to make sure that the loaves do not burn. Check the base of each loaf with a tap of your finger — if it sounds hollow, it is ready. Baking should take no longer than 40 minutes in total.

yeasted breads

Apart from the brioche, all of the following yeasted breads contain a combination of fresh yeast and white starter as the leavening agent. Semi-sourdough loaves contain a little of the sourness and texture of a sourdough, but with a more airy, open crumb. While a pure sourdough takes a long time to prove and has a thick chewy crust, yeasted doughs take less time to prove and have thin, crisp crusts. The combination of white starter and commercial yeast combines the best of both worlds, resulting in a quicker production time and a lighter, child-friendly loaf, with the flavour and texture of sourdough.

ingredients

540 g (1 lb 3 oz) white starter (see pages 42–5)
680 g (1 lb 8 oz) organic plain flour
10 g (¼ oz) fresh yeast
275 ml (9½ fl oz) water
12 g (⅓ oz/1¼ tablespoons) sea salt

This is the loaf that epitomises the balance between new and old worlds, using both commercial yeast and sourdough starter. The versatility of this dough is impressive — it can be shaped into regular loaves, baguettes or small rolls (see pages 100–3) and makes the perfect fairy bread.

white semi-sourdough

makes 1.5 kg (3 lb 5 oz) dough or 3 loaves

method

To mix the semi-sourdough by hand, put the starter in a large mixing bowl with the flour, yeast and water. Stir with a large spoon until the mixture comes together to form a dough. Turn out onto a clean work surface and knead into a ball with your hands, for about 10 minutes. Cover with plastic wrap and set aside to rest for 20 minutes. Sprinkle the salt over the dough and knead it for a further 5 minutes. Cover and set aside for 10 minutes. Knead well for a further 5 minutes or until smooth and elastic.

If you are using an electric mixer, put the starter in the bowl of the mixer with a dough hook attachment. Add the flour, yeast, water and salt. Mix on slow speed for 4 minutes, then scrape down the sides of the bowl. Increase the speed to high for 5 minutes, or until the dough comes away from the edges of the bowl and is smooth and elastic.

If the dough tears at the slightest touch, it is under-mixed and you need to mix it more — what you want is to be able to stretch out the dough to transparency and create a window. Cover the bowl and set aside to rest for 20 minutes.

Lightly grease a container with oil spray and sit the dough inside. Cover with plastic wrap and set aside at ambient room temperature (approximately 20°C/68°F) for 1 hour to bulk prove.

To knock back the dough, turn it out onto a lightly floured surface and press out into a rectangle, about 2.5 cm (1 inch) thick. Use your hands to fold one-third back onto itself, then repeat with the remaining third. Turn the dough 90 degrees and fold it over again into thirds. Place the dough back into the oiled container and continue to bulk prove for a further 1 hour.

The dough is now ready to be divided, rested and shaped into your desired loaves. Use a blunt knife or divider to divide the dough into three even-sized portions, about 500 g (1 lb 2 oz) each. Working with one portion of dough at a time, surround the dough with your cupped hands, always keeping your hands in contact with the dough. In an anti-clockwise motion, start rolling the dough to create a tight ball with a smooth surface. Set aside on a lightly floured surface for 20 minutes, covered with plastic wrap.

Lightly grease three 15 x 9 cm (6 x 3½ inch) loaf (bar) tins, about 10 cm (4 inches) deep. Working with one ball of dough at a time, stretch each dough portion out to double its width. Fold a third into itself towards the middle, then fold in the other third to overlap in the middle. Then, as if you are building a paper aeroplane, fold it in to create the nose cone at the end furthest from the edge of the bench. Press this down to prevent any large air pockets forming.

Bring the dough into the shape that will be placed into the tin. With your fingers tensed, press down onto the nose cone and fold inwards keeping the action tight — this is called crimping. Use small movements with your fingers, folding over the dough and pressing down as you work to create tension and form. Crimp with your fingers until you reach halfway into the dough, then with the ball of your dominant hand press down against the seam closing it into the dough. Continue this motion with both hands, folding the dough over in tight movements, each time closing the seam. Check to see that the seam is straight and closed; if not, pinch the seam to close it. Place the dough in the tins and cover loosely with plastic wrap. Alternatively, you can place the loaves on a baking tray lined with baking paper, seam side down. Place the dough in the refrigerator for 1 hour.

Preheat the oven to its highest temperature. Remove the loaves from the refrigerator and let them rest in a humid place, about 25°C (77°F) — this could take anywhere between 30 minutes and 1½ hours — until each loaf has grown in size by two-thirds. If the loaves push back steadily and quickly when you push lightly into them with a finger then they are ready.

Spray the oven with water and bake for 20 minutes, then turn the loaves or trays around, and bake for a further 10 minutes. Check the base of each loaf with a tap of your finger — if it sounds hollow, it is ready. The loaves should take no longer than 40 minutes in total to bake.

1.5 kg (3 lb 5 oz) white semi-sourdough dough (see pages 98–9)

A traditional baguette commonly weighs 250 g (9 oz) and is 6 cm (2½ inches) wide with the length varying from anywhere up to 100 cm (39½ inches) long! The baguette size you decide upon will obviously be determined by your oven and tray. Baguettes should have a crisp crust without a dry interior. which means a short bake at a high temperature. You can also adapt this recipe to make rolls and mini baguettes.

baguettes

makes 7 baguettes

method

To make baguettes, follow the instructions for mixing the white semi-sourdough on pages 98–9, until you can create a window. Use a blunt knife or divider to divide the dough into seven even-sized portions, each weighing 200 g (7 oz) each. Shape into balls, place on a floured tray and set aside to rest for 20 minutes.

Working with one ball of dough at a time, flatten it out with the palm of your hand. Fold the flattened piece of dough into itself in thirds, pressing down evenly. Turn the dough so that the folded seam is facing you and start crimping the dough on the side furthest away from you. To crimp the dough, use your fingertips to pull the dough over towards you, pushing it down and inwards in one movement (see pictures opposite and over). Repeat this process another three times to create more tension. Use the ball of your hand to push down along the seam and repeat the crimping until you have almost made a cylinder. Seal the seam using the ball of your hand to press along the dough seam — you will hear popping sounds when the seam is totally closed. When you turn the cylinder over, the seam should be in a straight line. Now it is time to roll out to a baguette.

Start with the palms of your hands together, lightly resting on the middle of the cylinder of dough. Push down and roll out with your hands to elongate the cylinder — make sure there are no divots, which may happen if one hand, usually your dominant hand, is pressing too firmly into the dough. Turn the baguette so it is seam side down. Repeat the process of rolling and checking the baguette until it is about 30 cm (12 inches) long and 5 cm (2 inches) wide.

1. Flatten each portion of dough with your hand to make a rectangular shape, making sure it is even all over.

2. Fold one-third of the dough to meet in the middle, then fold the other third over the top.

3. Turn the dough so the seam faces you and use your fingertips to pull the dough towards you, pushing down and inwards as you work.

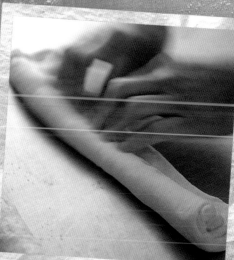

4. Keep your fingers tense as you crimp along the baguette.

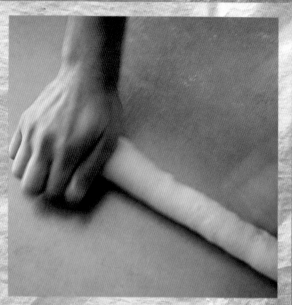

5. Seal the seam with the ball of your hand to make a straight line — a popping sound will indicate when the seam is totally closed.

6. Roll the baguettes out using both hands, trying to keep the pressure as even as possible.

7. Lay the rolled baguettes wedged between a tea towel (dish towel) dusted with flour, with the seam side facing up. Set aside to rest for 20 minutes before scoring and baking.

To make the pointy ends, press the ends firmly with your hands, squeezing the dough into thin points. Repeat with the remaining dough to make seven baguettes in total.

Preheat the oven to its highest temperature. At Bourke Street Bakery we prove our baguettes on couche (Belgium linen). At home, you can place a tea towel (dish towel) lengthways on a baking tray and sprinkle flour liberally over the cloth. Place a baguette, seam side up, at one edge of the tea towel, pushing the wide edge of the tea towel slightly over the baguette to form a barrier between the next baguette you lay down. Keep dusting the towel with flour before you lay down each baguette. When you have placed all the baguettes on the tray, cover loosely with a plastic bag and set aside in a warm place (25°C/77°F) to prove for 30 minutes.

To check that the baguettes are ready to cook, press one gently with your finger — it should bounce back. Gently roll each baguette out of the tea towel so the seam side is facing down. Transfer the baguette onto a baking tray lined with baking paper, seam side down.

To slash a baguette you need a very sharp knife. Pinch the baguette gently with your hand, then with your knife in the other hand, make five or six 6 cm (2½ inch) diagonal incisions along the middle of the baguette at regular intervals. On each following incision, overlap it by a third to create what is known as the bridge. Try not to fuss over your slashing too much. See where you want to cut your baguette and just do it. This is not one of those actions that benefits from a long slow agonising process. Having said that, you still need to concentrate.

Place the baguettes in the oven and spray the oven with water. Bake for 10 minutes, then turn the trays around and check that the bases are not burning, and bake for a further 10–15 minutes.

variation

To make semi-sourdough rolls you can make baguettes, let them rest and then slice each baguette on an angle into five pieces, creating diamond-shaped rolls.

If you want a round roll, you need to divide the dough into 60 g (2¼ oz) weights after the dough has been mixed and bulk proved, then leave them to rest for 20 minutes. Shape them into balls in the cup of your hand and place them on trays to prove for 30 minutes.

If you want tiny little baguettes you can pre-shape the dough into balls of your desired weight and let them rest for 20 minutes. Follow the directions on how to shape a baguette. Place them directly onto trays lined with baking paper. Bake the rolls and small baguettes for 10 minutes, then turn the tray and cook for a further 5 minutes if required.

260 g (9¼ oz) white starter (see pages 42–5)

40 g (1½ oz) rye starter (see pages 43–5)

145 g (5¼ oz) organic plain flour

375 g (13 oz) organic rye flour

10 g (¼ oz) fresh yeast

12 g (⅓ oz/1¼ tablespoons) sea salt

300 ml (10½ fl oz) water

Light rye bread is a really healthy, flavoursome loaf that keeps well for at least a week after baking. This recipe uses 72 per cent rye flour, so the remaining white flour has the ability to be developed but the rye flour does not. The mixing times are shorter than other yeasted breads to reflect this.

light rye bread

makes 2 loaves

method

To mix the light rye dough by hand, put the white and rye starters in a large mixing bowl with the white and rye flours, yeast, sea salt and water. Mix together with a large spoon until the mixture comes together to form a dough, about 10 minutes. Turn out onto a clean work surface and knead into a ball with your hands for about 15 minutes, or until smooth but slightly sticky.

If you are using an electric mixer, put the white and rye starters in the bowl of the electric mixer with the dough hook attachment. Add the white and rye flours, yeast, sea salt and water. Mix on slow speed for 7 minutes. Scrape down the sides of the bowl then continue mixing on high speed for 3 minutes, or until smooth.

Lightly grease a container with oil spray and sit the dough inside. Cover with plastic wrap and set aside at ambient room temperature (approximately 20°C/68°F) for 1 hour to bulk prove.

To knock back the dough, turn it out onto a lightly floured surface and press out into a rectangle, about 2.5 cm (1 inch) thick. Use your hands to fold one-third back onto itself, then repeat with the remaining third. Turn the dough 90 degrees and fold it over again into thirds. Place the dough back into the oiled container and continue to bulk prove for a further 1 hour.

Use a blunt knife or divider to divide the dough into two even-sized portions, about 500 g (1 lb 2 oz) each. Working with one portion of dough at a time, continue to shape the loaves as for a batard on pages 30–5.

Preheat the oven to its highest temperature. Place the loaves on a baking tray and dust lightly with rye flour. Score the loaves; with a high percentage of rye flour this loaf can be scored before the final prove. Scoring the loaf at this stage will not restrict its ability to prove up, but rather allow it to grow and fill the void left by your deft cuts. Set aside in a warm place (25°C/77°F) to prove for 40 minutes.

Place the loaves in the oven and spray the oven with water. Reduce the temperature to 220°C (425°F/Gas 7). Bake the loaves for 30 minutes, then turn the trays around and bake for a further 10–15 minutes, or until a deep brown — you should also hear a dull hollow sound when you tap the base of the loaves.

ingredients

125 g (4½ oz) desiree potatoes, cut into 3 cm (1¼ inch) cubes
20 ml (½ fl oz/1 tablespoon) olive oil
110 g (3¾ oz) white starter (see pages 42–5)
225 g (8 oz) organic wholemeal (whole-wheat) flour
225 g (8 oz) organic plain flour
8 g (¼ oz/3 teaspoons) sea salt
5 g (⅛ oz) fresh yeast
300 ml (10½ fl oz) water
4 rosemary sprigs, leaves picked

This was the original potato bread before it grew up into a sourdough. Its texture is lighter and wholesome and far more innocent and care-free. All that changed with the addition of nigella seeds and the omission of the wholemeal flour. The sourdough Mr Potato Bread (see page 92–5) has a chewier crumb with a thicker crust but is a far more flavoursome loaf with nigella seeds, which becomes the dominant flavour. This loaf is beautifully simple, showcasing the potato and rosemary.

potato bread junior

makes 2 loaves

method

Preheat the oven to 220°C (425°F/Gas 7). Put the potato cubes in a baking tray and pour over the oil. Season with salt and freshly ground black pepper and bake in the oven for 15 minutes, or until you can almost pierce them all the way through with a knife — the potatoes only need to be half-cooked at this stage as they will continue cooking when the loaf is baked. If the potatoes are overcooked they will disintegrate when you go to fold them through the dough. Imperfection is often the signature of a handmade product. If it has potatoes spilling out when you cut the loaf, you know only the human hand could have achieved that.

To mix the potato bread by hand, put the white starter in a large bowl with the wholemeal and plain flours, sea salt, yeast and water. Mix together with a large spoon until the mixture comes together to form a dough, about 5 minutes. Turn out onto a clean work surface and knead into a ball with your hands for about 15 minutes, or until smooth.

If you are using an electric mixer, put the white starter in the bowl of the mixer with the dough hook attachment. Add the wholemeal and plain flours, sea salt, yeast and water. Mix on slow speed for 4 minutes. Scrape down the sides of the bowl then continue mixing on high speed for 6 minutes or until smooth (it will not be elastic).

When the dough is properly developed fold through the potatoes and rosemary, either by hand or very gently on the slowest setting of your mixer.

Lightly grease a container with oil spray and sit the dough inside. Cover with plastic wrap and set aside at ambient room temperature (approximately 20°C/68°F) for 1 hour to bulk prove.

To knock back the dough, turn it out onto a lightly floured surface and press out into a rectangle, about 2.5 cm (1 inch) thick. Use your hands to fold one-third back onto itself, then repeat with the remaining third. Turn the dough 90 degrees and fold it over again into thirds. Place the dough back into the oiled container and continue to bulk prove for a further 30 minutes.

Use a blunt knife or divider to divide the dough into two even-sized portions, about 500 g (1 lb 2 oz) each. Working with one portion of dough at a time, continue to shape the loaves following the instructions for shaping a round loaf on pages 30–5.

Line two small baskets with a tea towel (dish towel) in each, lightly dust both with flour and place a loaf inside each, seam side up. If you are using a traditional cane basket, you don't need the tea towel and can simply dust the basket with flour. Alternatively, you can place the loaves on a baking tray lined with baking paper, seam side down. Place in the refrigerator loosely covered with a plastic bag for 1 hour.

Preheat the oven to its highest temperature. Remove the loaves from the refrigerator and let them rest in a humid place (25°C/77°F) — this could take anywhere between 1 and 4 hours — until each loaf has grown in size by two-thirds. If the loaves push back steadily and quickly when you push lightly into them with a finger then they are ready. Score the loaves (see page 39) and place them in the oven.

Spray the oven with water and reduce the temperature to 220°C (425°F/Gas 7). Bake the loaves for 20 minutes, then turn the loaves or trays around, and bake for a further 10 minutes, watching carefully to make sure that the loaves do not burn. Check the base of each loaf with a tap of your finger — if it sounds hollow, it is ready. Baking should take no longer than 40 minutes in total.

ingredients

40 g (1½ oz) white starter (see pages 42–5)
110 g (3¾ oz) organic rye flour
340 g (12 oz) organic plain flour
2½ tablespoons plain yoghurt
250 ml (9 fl oz/1 cup) water
10 g (¼ oz) fresh yeast
1 tablespoon soft brown sugar
10 g (¼ oz/1 tablespoon) sea salt
165 g (5¾ oz) green apples, peeled, cored and cut into
2–3 cm (¾–1¼ inch) cubes
2 teaspoons ground cinnamon

This tasty loaf should have a fairly open crumb and a cinnamon aroma. You should be able to taste the sweetness of the brown sugar and apples, a hint of sourness from the yoghurt and an earthiness from the rye flour.

apple, yoghurt, rye and cinnamon loaf

makes 2 loaves

method

To mix the apple, yoghurt, rye and cinnamon loaf by hand, put the white starter in a large bowl with the rye and plain flours, yoghurt, water, yeast, sugar and sea salt. Mix together with a large spoon until the mixture comes together to form a dough, about 5 minutes. Turn out onto a clean work surface and knead into a ball with your hands for about 15 minutes, or until smooth.

If you are using an electric mixer, put the starter, rye and plain flours, yoghurt and water into the bowl of the mixer fitted with a dough hook attachment. Add the crumbled yeast, brown sugar and salt. Mix on slow speed for 4 minutes, then increase the speed to high and continue mixing for 6 minutes.

When the dough is properly developed fold through the diced apples and cinnamon, either by hand or very gently on the slowest setting of your mixer.

Lightly grease a container with oil spray and sit the dough inside. Cover with plastic wrap and set aside at ambient room temperature (approximately 20°C/68°F) for 30 minutes to bulk prove.

To knock back the dough, turn it out onto a lightly floured surface and press out into a rectangle, about 2.5 cm (1 inch) thick. Use your hands to fold one-third back onto itself, then repeat with the remaining third. Turn the dough 90 degrees and fold it over again into thirds. Place the dough back into the oiled container and continue to bulk prove for a further 30 minutes.

Use a blunt knife or divider to divide the dough into two even-sized portions, about 500 g (1 lb 2 oz). Working with one portion of dough at a time, continue to shape the loaves as for a round loaf on pages 30–5. Place the loaves on a baking tray lined with baking paper, seam side down. Place in the refrigerator loosely covered with a plastic bag for 1 hour.

Preheat the oven to its highest temperature. Remove the loaves from the refrigerator and let them rest in a humid place (25°C/77°F) — this could take anywhere between 30 minutes and 1½ hours — until each loaf has grown in size by two-thirds. If the loaves push back steadily and quickly when you push lightly into them with a finger then they are ready. Score the loaves (see page 39) and place them in the oven.

Spray the oven with water and reduce the temperature to 220°C (425°F/Gas 7). Bake the loaves for 20 minutes, then turn the loaves or trays around, and bake for a further 10 minutes, watching carefully to make sure that the loaves do not burn. Check the base of each loaf with a tap of your finger — if it sounds hollow, it is ready. Baking should take no longer than 40 minutes in total.

190 g (6¾ oz) plain (all-purpose) flour, chilled

4 g (⅛ oz) fresh yeast, chilled

15 g (½ oz) caster (superfine) sugar, chilled

30 ml (1 fl oz/1½ tablespoons) milk, chilled

3 eggs, chilled

5 g (⅛ oz/1 teaspoon) salt

125 g (4½ oz) unsalted butter, cut into 1.5 cm (⅝ inch) cubes, at room temperature, plus extra for greasing

egg wash (see page 168), for brushing

brioche

makes 1 loaf

Brioche is a very indulgent bread. Or is it a cake? It's possibly best described as a yeast-risen cake, yet it can be savoury or sweet. Be it bread or cake this brioche recipe is one that you have to bake at least once. This dough is quite sticky and unable to be shaped into the classic fluted brioche moulds, but that is the beauty of this recipe, plenty of eggs and masses of butter resulting in a luscious, rich product. It is baked in a loaf tin and is best eaten thickly sliced and toasted, or topped with poached fruit and ice cream or custard to make a fabulous dessert. Serve it with jam and ricotta for breakfast or with sautéed mushrooms or pâté as an elegant entrée.

method

Preheat the oven to 220°C (425°F/Gas 7). Grease and line a 22 x 7.5 x 7.5 cm (8½ x 3 x 3 inch) loaf (bar) tin. Put the flour, yeast, sugar, milk, eggs and salt into the bowl of an electric mixer fitted with a dough hook. Mix on low speed for 3 minutes, then increase the speed to high and mix for another 3 minutes. Reduce the speed to medium and with the motor running, add a few pieces of butter at a time, making sure it is well incorporated before adding more — when finished the dough should be smooth, soft and very sticky to the point of being difficult to handle. You will find it easier when handling the dough to lightly dust the work surface and your hands with flour while you work.

Transfer the dough to a bowl that has been lightly greased with butter and cover with a clean tea towel (dish towel). Place in the refrigerator to prove for about 1 hour.

Turn the dough out onto a lightly floured work surface. Press the dough down, gently knocking out most of the air inside and pressing out to form a rectangle, about 2.5 cm (1 inch) thick. Use your hands to fold one-third back onto itself, then repeat with the remaining third. Turn the dough 90 degrees and fold it over again into thirds. Place the dough back into the container, making sure the folds are underneath, cover, and continue to bulk prove in the refrigerator for a further 1 hour.

Turn the dough out onto a lightly floured work surface and gently knock out the air again. Press the dough out into a rectangle and fold the two sides to your left and right into the centre. The dough should be as wide as the tin is long. Press the dough down to form a rectangle and starting from the side furthest away from you, roll the dough towards you to form a log. Use the palm of your hand to close the seam running the length of the log. Place the dough into the tin, seam side down. Brush the top of the loaf with egg wash. Reduce the oven temperature to 180°C (350°F/Gas 4). Bake the brioche for about 40 minutes, or until golden — when turned out of the tin and tapped on the base it should sound hollow.

olive oil breads

Olive oil dough is fantastically versatile. It most resembles a ciabatta dough with a few minor changes. A basic olive oil dough recipe can be adapted and used to make panini, flatbreads, pizza dough, schiacciata or grissini.

Olive oil dough contains milk, extra virgin olive oil and also relies on a ferment (in this case day-old dough), which is added to the mix halfway through. The milk helps to preserve the loaf and also makes the interior crumb consistent. The extra virgin olive oil acts as a preserving agent and adds flavour. The ferment helps in a couple of ways. It has a role in aiding proving, but its main purpose is to change the texture and flavour of the dough. Without the ferment, the dough would be lighter and airier. With ferment added, the bread will have a denser, slightly sour crumb. You may prefer not making the ferment for your first dough and trying the lighter version instead. In any case, it will give you a chance to compare a dough with ferment and one without.

An olive oil loaf should have a thin crust with an interior crumb that is soft. When you go to slice a piece to toast, you should not end up with large holes where the jam disappears. With an elastic dough such as this one, it is possible to have a very high water percentage. This dough is made with strong flour, which unlike all our sourdoughs, is non-organic; the strands are able to stretch further and absorb more water, thereby increasing the yield.

Once the loaves are baked, some of the water evaporates and you are left with quite a crusty loaf, which is fine if this is the result you want. At Bourke Street Bakery we strive for a soft, child-friendly loaf. As preferences vary, it is important to be aware of how each ingredient can change and shape the loaf, so that you can manipulate the results to make the best loaf for you.

ingredients

100 g (3½ oz) strong flour
2½ g (⅟₁₆ oz/1 teaspoon) sea salt
¾ teaspoon extra virgin olive oil
½ teaspoon milk
70 ml (2¼ fl oz) water
2 g (⅟₁₆ oz) fresh yeast

Here is the ferment recipe if you wish to use ferment in your first olive oil dough. After this, you will never need to make ferment again, as you can keep recycling a little of the old olive oil dough and use it as ferment. Its role is not primarily as a rising agent, so if your ferment is two or three days old, it is still okay to use. If it's older than this, it is best to make a new ferment. Always keep your ferment in the fridge. It is possible to freeze ferment that you wish to use in later doughs — be sure to freeze in recipe batches and thaw a day before use.

first or initial ferment

makes 180 g (6¼ oz)

method

To mix the ferment by hand put all the ingredients in a bowl and stir together to combine, about 5 minutes. If you are using an electric mixer, put all of the ingredients in the bowl of the mixer on low speed for 2 minutes. Increase the speed to high and continue mixing for 5 minutes, or until the dough is smooth and elastic. Transfer the dough to a container that has been sprayed with olive oil. Cover with plastic wrap and rest overnight in the refrigerator before using.

ingredients

600 g (1 lb 5 oz) strong flour

13 g (½ oz) fresh yeast

400 ml (14 fl oz) water

20 ml (1 fl oz) extra virgin olive oil

20 ml (1 fl oz) milk

15 g (½ oz/1½ tablespoons) sea salt

180 g (6¼ oz) ferment (see page 121), (optional)

This recipe makes two loaves with enough left-over dough to use as ferment for the next mix. Olive oil dough is very wet and hard to mix by hand. If you do have an electric mixer now is the time to use it. Automated mixing is easier and will give you consistently better results, but you will gain a better appreciation of how the dough is changing and developing if you mix a dough by hand first. Letting the dough rest between mixes and adding an additional knock back, will help improve your chances of a well-developed dough.

Once you have mixed the basic olive oil dough you can also use it to make paninis, flatbreads, schiacciata, grissini or the chorizo and thyme rolls on the following pages.

olive oil dough

makes 1 kg (2 lb 4 oz) of dough or 2 loaves

method

To mix the olive oil dough by hand, put the flour and yeast in a large bowl and pour in the water. Use a spoon to mix together until well combined, then set aside for 10 minutes. Add the oil, milk and salt, mixing well. Turn the dough out onto a lightly floured work surface and start kneading. Knead for 10 minutes, then allow the dough to rest for 10 minutes. Add the ferment (if using) and knead for a further 10 minutes.

If you are using an electric mixer, put all of the ingredients, except the ferment, into the bowl of the mixer fitted with a dough hook. Mix on low speed for 2 minutes, then increase the speed to high and continue mixing for 5 minutes. If using the ferment break it up with your hands and scatter into the bowl. Continue mixing on low speed for 1 minute, then increase the speed to high and mix for 5 minutes, or until well combined — this may take an extra couple of minutes — the dough should come away from the edges of the bowl and have a silky complexion when done.

Place the dough in a container that has been sprayed with olive oil, cover with plastic wrap and set aside to bulk prove for 1½ hours. Knock back the dough every 30 minutes during the bulk prove — this means you will need to knock back the dough twice in total.

To knock back the dough, turn it out onto a lightly floured surface and press out into a rectangle, about 2.5 cm (1 inch) thick. Use your hands to fold one third back onto itself, then repeat with the remaining third. Turn the dough ninety degrees and fold it over again into thirds. Place the dough back into the oiled container, cover with plastic wrap, and continue to bulk prove for a further 1 hour. Once the dough has finished to bulk prove it is ready to be divided and shaped.

Turn the dough out onto a lightly floured surface. Press the dough evenly into a 20 cm (8 inch) square block. Use a divider or blunt knife to cut the dough into even halves. Trim both halves into oblongs — they should weigh 500 g (1 lb 2 oz) each. If you horribly miscalculate the size of a loaf you can add to the weight by stretching a piece of dough and pinching it onto either end of the loaf. Make sure that when you place it on the tray it is renovated side down. The trimmings that litter your bench are now ferment that can be used for tomorrow's loaves. Place the ferment in a container that has been sprayed with olive oil, cover with plastic wrap and refrigerate overnight.

Place the loaves on baking trays lined with baking paper. Dust with a little flour, and set aside in a warm, humid place (25°C/77°F) to prove for about 40 minutes depending on the climate of the room — the loaves should have risen by two-thirds and should bounce back when pushed. The dough should look airy and spongy — on a good day, a good dough should look like spun silk.

Preheat the oven to its highest temperature. Place the loaves in the oven and spray the oven with water. Bake for 20 minutes, then turn the loaves around and bake for a further 10 minutes, watching carefully to make sure that the loaves do not burn. Tap the base of the loaves with your fingers and listen — if they sound hollow the loaves are ready. Baking should not take longer than 40 minutes in total.

The panino is a filled bread roll — basically a sandwich for those of us who are not protecting a heritage. Panini (more than one panino) are all about kids — they are little rolls for little hands and are easy to cut to size and fill with your choice of filling.

panini makes 30

method

To make panini, follow the instructions for making olive oil dough on pages 122–3. To divide and shape the panini, turn the dough out onto a lightly floured work surface and press down until it is about 5 cm (2 inches) high. Roll out the dough to about 2 cm (¾ inch) thick all over — the dough should be smooth with no dimples in the surface. Flip up half of the dough onto itself and dust the bench underneath with flour. Lay the dough back down on the floured bench. Repeat with the other half of the dough. This will ensure the dough does not stick when you start to divide the rolls. Let the dough rest for 5–10 minutes so it can shrink back to its correct shape.

Cut the dough lengthways into 4 cm (1½ inch) wide strips, then cut each strip at 4 cm (1½ inch) intervals to make neat squares. You can use 180 g (6¼ oz) of these trimmings as ferment for the next dough or freeze for the next dough. To make round panini, use a pastry cutter with a 4 cm (1½ inch) diameter.

Preheat the oven to its highest setting. Place the panini on baking trays lined with baking paper, dust with a little flour or semolina. Set aside in a warm, humid place (25°C/77°F) to prove for about 20–30 minutes. Once proved, the panini should have risen by one-third and look like taut fluffy pillows. When you push a finger into them, they should spring back and not deflate. If they are sagging they are over-proved.

Place the panini in the oven and spray the oven with water. Bake for 10 minutes then, depending on the size of your panini, you may need to turn the tray and bake for a further 5–10 minutes, or until they have grown by one-third and are golden brown.

Flatbread seems to be a weekend affair at the bakery. Needing no sharp implements to dissect, it is the loaf most likely to be shared with friends (or eaten on the way home) as it is already topped with flavour. It's also great for picnics or mezze-style lunches.

Once you have mixed the olive oil dough, you need to add the toppings halfway through the proving stage – once the dough has had time to prove without being weighed down with ingredients, but not so long that when you do add the ingredients the flatbread deflates. It is best to keep the toppings simple and only use two to four different ingredients. Some of the more popular combinations have been included below, but we are also fond of green olive flatbread, anchovy and oregano flatbread or herb and olive flatbread using tarragon, chives, oregano, thyme and even nigella seeds.

flatbreads makes 2 flatbreads

method

To make flatbread, follow the instructions for mixing olive oil dough on pages 122–3. Once the dough has finished its bulk prove, you can shape the flatbread.

Turn the dough out onto a lightly floured work surface and press down evenly with your hands, until it is a rectangle about 25 x 10 cm (10 x 4 inches) and 2 cm (¾ inch) high. Divide the dough into two even-sized portions, about 500 g (1 lb 2 oz) each, trimming each flatbread to create a 25 x 5 cm (10 x 2 inch) rectangular shape. Remember, if you wish to make another olive oil dough you will need to wrap 180 g (6¼ oz) of ferment in plastic wrap and store it in the refrigerator.

Place each flatbread on a baking tray lined with baking paper and use your fingers to press down into the dough and create shallow indents over the surface. Set aside in a warm place (25°C/77°F) to prove for 15 minutes.

Add the topping of your choice and set aside to prove for a further 15–20 minutes. Preheat the oven to 180°C (350°F/Gas 4). Place in the oven and spray the oven with water. Bake for 25–30 minutes, turning the flatbread around after 15 minutes. Remove from the oven and leave to cool until you can safely eat it.

rosemary and olive topping

ingredients
20 ml (½ fl oz/1 tablespoon) extra virgin olive oil
2 rosemary sprigs, leaves picked
100 g (3½ oz/⅔ cup) roughly chopped pitted black olives

method
Brush each flatbread with the extra virgin olive oil. Scatter half the olives down each flatbread and sprinkle half of the rosemary over each. Sprinkle with some freshly ground black pepper.

smoked paprika and capsicum topping

ingredients
1 green capsicum (pepper), seeded, membrane removed
and cut into 3 cm (1¼ inch) pieces
1 yellow capsicum (pepper), seeded, membrane removed
and cut into 3 cm (1¼ inch) pieces
1 red capsicum (pepper), seeded, membrane removed
and cut into 3 cm (1¼ inch) pieces
1½ teaspoons smoked paprika
55 ml (1¾ fl oz) extra virgin olive oil

method
Preheat the oven to 200°C (400°F/Gas 6). Toss the capsicums together in a bowl with a pinch of salt and freshly ground black pepper. Spread out on a baking tray and cook in the oven for 30 minutes, or until tender. Allow to cool. Sprinkle the paprika into the oil and brush over each flatbread. Grab a handful of the cooled roasted capsicum and press the pieces into the flatbreads so that they are half submerged in the dough.

sumac and roast garlic topping

This garlic recipe takes a few hours to prepare but it will last for at least 1 month submerged in oil in the refrigerator. You can use the garlic confit in everyday cooking and it is great to have on hand as it imparts a sweet garlic flavour in casseroles and soups and is great for stuffing meat or chicken.

ingredients
500 g (1 lb 2 oz) garlic cloves, halved
500 ml (17 fl oz/2 cups) olive oil
3 teaspoons sumac
55 ml (1¾ fl oz) extra virgin olive oil

method
To make the pure garlic confit, put the garlic and olive oil in a heavy-based saucepan over low heat and simmer for 3 hours or until just tender. Set aside to cool. Sprinkle the sumac into the oil and brush over each flatbread. Take 6 tablespoons of garlic and press into each flatbread, submerging and pinching the dough to cover the garlic.

cherry tomato, parmesan and basil topping

ingredients
20 cherry tomatoes, halved
50 g (1¾ oz) parmesan cheese, roughly chopped
1 large handful basil leaves, torn
55 ml (1¾ fl oz) extra virgin olive oil

method
Press the tomato halves and parmesan into each flatbread until half submerged. The tomatoes look best when facing cut side up. You can either press the basil leaves into the flatbread at this point and brush the extra virgin olive oil on top or you can put the basil in a food processor or blender with the extra virgin olive oil, and blend until just spreadable but not runny. If using the basil oil, brush it over the flatbreads when they come out of the oven.

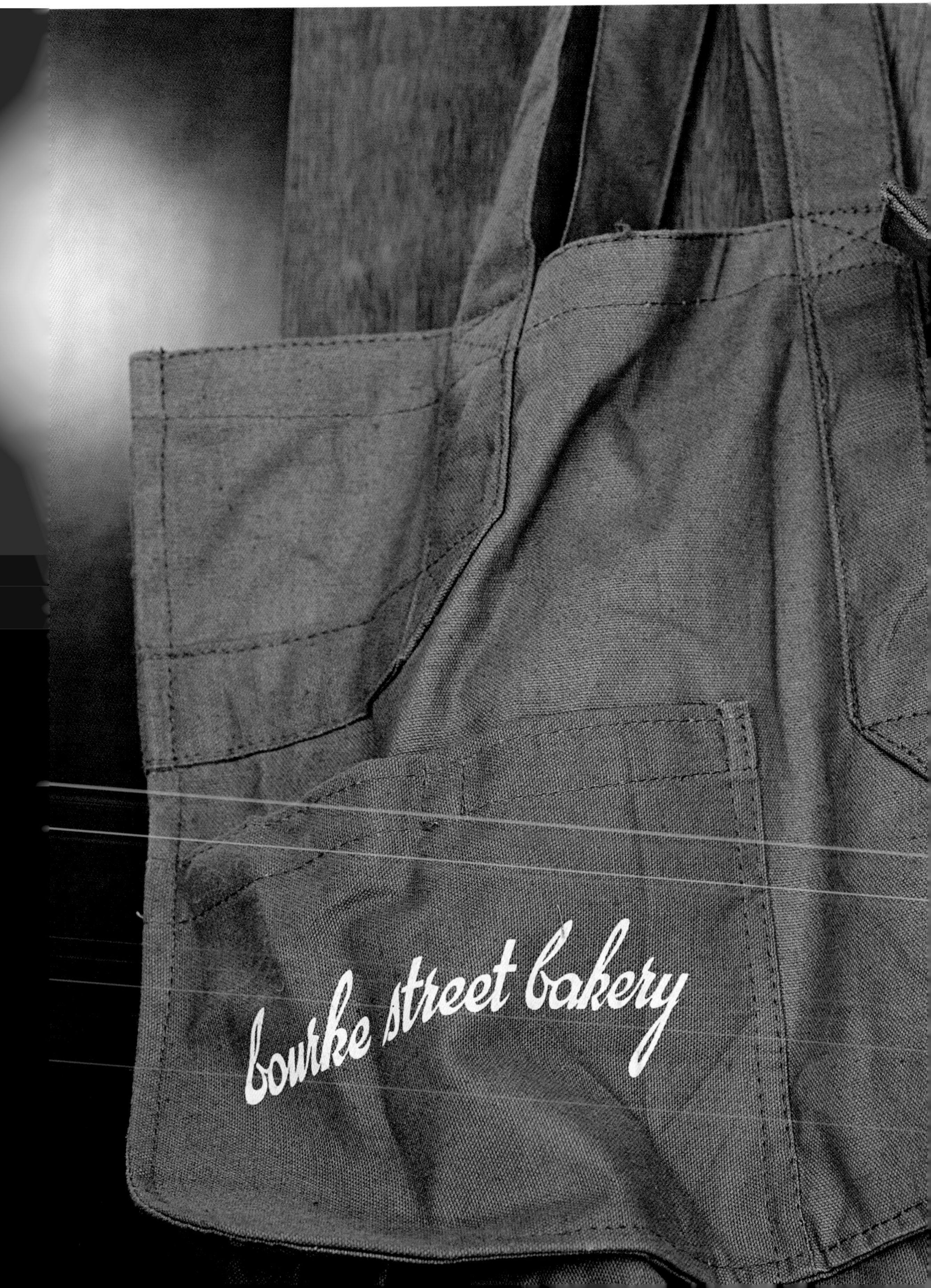
bourke street bakery

ingredients

400 g (14 oz) olive oil dough (see pages 122–3)
500 g (1 lb 2 oz) black seedless grapes
2 rosemary sprigs, leaves picked and roughly chopped
raw (demerara) sugar (optional)

We use the olive oil dough for the base of this Italian classic. We never make this out of season as it relies on good grapes to do it justice. We used regular black grapes in the first few attempts but due to a 'public seed backlash' changed to black seedless grapes instead.

grape schiacciata

makes 2

method

To make schiacciata, follow the instructions for making olive oil dough on pages 122–3. Once the dough has finished its bulk prove, you can shape the schiacciata.

Divide the dough into two even-sized portions. Use a rolling pin to roll out each portion to create a 30 x 15 cm (12 x 6 inch) rectangle, about 5 mm (¼ inch) thick all over, making sure you let the dough rest between each roll for a couple of minutes. Gently transfer the dough to a baking tray lined with baking paper. Set aside in a warm place (25°C/77°F) to prove for 20 minutes.

Preheat the oven to 220°C (425°F/Gas 7). Pick and wash the grapes and place in a bowl. Crush them roughly with your fists to get some of the juice out. (Do not pound them to a paste, as you still want to see that they are grapes.) Drain the juice. Check the dough with a prod of your finger; it should rise back steadily and look puffy and glossy.

Scatter the grapes over the dough, leaving a 5 mm (¼ inch) border around the edges. Sprinkle the rosemary on top and then the sugar, if using.

Reduce the oven temperature to 200°C (400°F/Gas 6) and bake for 25 minutes, turning after 10 minutes. This bread does not need steaming as there is already a lot of moisture coming from the grapes. It's important to check the base to see it is cooked all the way through. Schiacciata is best cooked on the hearth, so if you have a pizza stone, this is the time to use it.

ingredients

caramelised onion (makes 510 g/1 lb 2 oz)

1.1 kg (2 lb 7 oz) brown onions, sliced

40 ml (1¼ fl oz/2 tablespoons)
olive oil

2 desiree potatoes

400 g (14 oz) olive oil dough
(see pages 122–3)

10 prosciutto slices (optional)

2 rosemary sprigs, leaves picked

A mandolin is just an update of the guillotine, but for a vegetable. It is a dangerous but invaluable tool for any kitchen. Even in professional kitchens people struggle to keep their fingers free from harm, but if you do master the mandolin, it will result in a superior product. To truly suffer for your art, you may have to lose a few fingers along the way.

potato schiacciata makes 2 loaves

method

To make the caramelised onions, heat the oil in a heavy-based saucepan over low heat. Add the onion and cook for 2 hours, stirring every 10 minutes, until the natural sugars caramelise and turn the onions brown. Allow to cool.

Use a mandolin or sharp knife to thinly slice the potatoes — they should be about 2 mm (1/16 inch) thick. Place them in a large bowl of water, then drain well. Put the potatoes in a saucepan, cover with water and simmer for 3–5 minutes, or until almost tender, then plunge into cold water until needed.

Meanwhile, follow the instructions for making olive oil dough on pages 122–3. To shape the dough, divide it into two even-sized portions. Roll out each portion to create a 30 x 15 cm (12 x 6 inch) rectangle, about 5 mm (¼ inch) thick all over, making sure you let the dough rest between each roll for a couple of minutes. Gently transfer the dough to a greased and lined tray. Leave to prove in a warm humid place (25°C/77°F) for 10 minutes.

Preheat the oven to 220°C (425°F/Gas 7). Spread a thin layer of caramelised onions over each piece of dough leaving a 1 cm (½ inch) border around the edges. Arrange the potato slices on top so they are slightly overlapping each other. If you are using prosciutto, lay the slices over the potato to cover evenly. Sprinkle the rosemary on top, season, and drizzle with a little extra virgin olive oil. Set aside to prove for a further 10 minutes.

Reduce the oven temperature to 200°C (400°F/Gas 6) and bake for 25 minutes, turning after 10 minutes. When cooked the schiacciata should have a crisp brown base and edge. If you added the prosciutto, it should be crisp.

1 kg (2 lb 4 oz) olive oil dough (see pages 122–3)

100 ml (3½ fl oz) olive oil

25 rosemary sprigs, leaves picked and chopped or

5 g (⅛ oz/2½ tablespoons) fennel seeds, ground

At Bourke Street Bakery we make grissini to use up any excess olive oil dough. They look great in the shop towering over the counter and are very simple to make, if a little fiddly. Stored in airtight containers they should keep for at least a week and are great with dips or as a snack for children.

grissini

makes 35–40

method

To make grissini, follow the instructions for making olive oil dough on pages 122–3. Once the dough has finished its bulk prove, you can divide and shape the grissini.

Turn the dough out onto a lightly floured work surface and use a rolling pin to roll it out to about 5 mm (¼ inch) thickness all over. Join together any dough that tears and let it rest for a couple of minutes before rolling it out again. Once you have achieved an even thickness let the dough rest for 5 minutes.

Preheat the oven to 170°C (325°F/Gas 3). Cut 1 cm (½ inch) strips lengthways along the dough to make grissini that are about 25–30 cm (10–12 inches) long. Lay them on a baking tray lined with baking paper and brush with oil. Sprinkle with the rosemary or ground fennel. Set aside in a warm place (25°C/77°F) for 20–30 minutes.

Reduce the oven temperature to 150°C (300°F/Gas 2) and cook them in the oven, without steam, for 30 minutes, or until pale and crisp.

ingredients

185 g (6½ oz) chorizo, cut into
1.5 cm (⅝ inch) cubes
250 g (9 oz/1 cup) caramelised onion
(see page 134)

6 thyme sprigs, leaves picked
2 teaspoons milk
1 kg (2 lb 4 oz) olive oil dough
(see pages 122–3)

This recipe uses the olive oil dough with roasted chorizo, thyme and caramelised onion folded through it. You can also make a vegetarian version of this roll by omitting the chorizo, or vary the mixture to suit your own tastes.

chorizo and thyme roll

makes 8 rolls

method

Preheat the oven to 200°C (400°F/Gas 6). Arrange the chorizo on baking trays lined with baking paper and cook for 5 minutes. Turn over and cook for a further 5 minutes. Set aside to cool completely.

In a bowl, mix together the chorizo and onion with their oils and add the thyme. Stir in the milk until well combined; set aside until needed.

Follow the instructions for making olive oil dough on pages 122–3. To shape the dough, turn it out onto a lightly floured work surface and roll it out into a 45 x 15 cm (17¾ x 6 inch) rectangle, about 1.5 cm (⅝ inch) thick. Lay the long side parallel with the edge of your work bench and mark the dough into thirds with your finger. Lay half of the chorizo mixture inside the middle third of the dough, spreading it evenly to the edges. Fold the right third of the dough over the middle and lightly press down to push out any air bubbles. Evenly spread the remaining chorizo mixture onto the folded third and fold over the left flap, lightly pressing down to seal.

Increase the oven temperature to 220°C (425°C/Gas 7). Use your fingers to mark the dough into thirds, this time parallel to the bench. Fold the top third over the middle third, then overlap with the bottom third. Press the dough down and leave to rest for 30 minutes.

Cut the dough into four strips, then cut each strip into two pieces. Place on a greased baking tray, then place in the oven and spray the oven with water. Reduce the oven temperature to 200°C (400°F/Gas 6) and cook for 20 minutes, turning the tray after 10 minutes, or until cooked and golden.

ingredients

600 g (1 lb 5 oz) strong flour
15 g ($\frac{1}{2}$ oz/3 teaspoons) sea salt
20 ml ($\frac{1}{2}$ fl oz/1 tablespoon) olive oil
15 ml ($\frac{1}{2}$ fl oz/3 teaspoons) milk
410 ml (14$\frac{1}{4}$ fl oz) water
10 g ($\frac{1}{4}$ oz) yeast

At Bourke Street Bakery we have created a pizza with a thin, crispy, subtle base. The recipe below is adapted from the olive oil dough — we simply increased the water content, olive oil and milk, lowered the amount of yeast and deleted the ferment altogether.

pizza dough makes 2 pizza bases

method

Put all of the ingredients into the bowl of an electric mixer. Mix on low speed for 3 minutes, then increase the speed to high and mix for 7 minutes, or until the dough comes away from the bowl and has a silky, smooth texture. Place the dough into a bowl that has been sprayed with olive oil. Cover with plastic wrap and set aside to prove for 20 minutes.

Preheat the oven to 220°C (425°F/Gas 7). Lightly grease two 36 x 26 cm (14$\frac{1}{4}$ x 10$\frac{1}{2}$ inch) rectangular oven trays. Divide the dough into two portions and use a rolling pin to roll each out to create two 40 x 30 cm (16 x 12 inch) rectangles, about 3 mm ($\frac{1}{8}$ inch) thick — you may need to do this in stages, allowing the dough to rest and relax between rolls. Gently transfer to the prepared trays, trimming the sides to fit the tray, and set aside for a couple of minutes.

Top the pizza bases with your favourite tomato sauce, mozzarella and one or two toppings. Set aside in a warm place (25°C/77°F) to prove for 15–20 minutes. Cook in the oven for about 15 minutes. If you have a pizza or hearth stone, slide the pizza bases onto the stone after 8 minutes; you will only need to cook them for a further 3 minutes each if using the stone.

At Bourke Street Bakery we cut and fold each piece of pizza so that we can toast them to order in a sandwich press, which makes for an easy snack on the go.

pastries

basics and techniques

Having the ability to make your own pastry has got to be one of the most satisfying achievements in the kitchen. You can produce a much better quality product than you can buy in any supermarket and after a few attempts you should find you can master most of the tasks fairly quickly.

Many things can go wrong when making and baking pastry so it is important to keep notes and be aware of each step so you can improve upon your efforts if things do go awry — persevering will lead to success. Don't be too worried about the look; short of burning the pastry or having the shell completely break, you can push ahead, as the result is bound to be tasty.

At Bourke Street Bakery we have adapted the following methods for mixing and rolling dough and lining pastry shells. If you are competent at making pastry and have methods and a style you are comfortable with, by all means go ahead with your own method. However, if you are new to pastry making, these tips will make your time in the kitchen easier.

ingredients

croissant ferment

100 g (3½ oz) strong flour, chilled

55 ml (1¾ fl oz) milk, chilled

5 g (⅛ oz/1 teaspoon) soft brown sugar, chilled

2½ g (1/16 oz ½ teaspoon) salt, chilled

5 g (⅛ oz) fresh yeast, chilled

20 g (¾ oz) unsalted butter, softened

935 g (2 lb 1 oz) strong flour, chilled

550 ml (19 fl oz) milk, chilled

60 g (2¼ oz/⅓ cup) soft brown sugar, chilled

15 g (½ oz/3 teaspoons) salt, chilled

35 g (1¼ oz) fresh yeast, chilled

500 g (1 lb 2 oz) unsalted butter, extra, for laminating, chilled

croissant dough

makes 1 quantity

Making croissant dough borrows more technique from making bread than from pastry. By allowing a croissant dough to prove slowly and adding a small amount of day-old-croissant dough (ferment) you can achieve a deeper more complex flavour. Careful folding of the dough (also known as laminating) will result in perfect thin layers of flaky pastry. Croissant dough is also used to make pan au chocolate, pan au raisin, danishes, bear claws and praline twists

method

To make the ferment, put all of the ingredients in a bowl and use one hand to squeeze everything together until the mixture starts to resemble a crumbly dough. Turn out onto a clean work surface and knead for about 10 minutes, or until you have a smooth elastic dough that doesn't break when stretched gently. If you are using an electric mixer, put all the ingredients in the bowl of the mixer fitted with a dough hook. Process on low speed for 3 minutes, or until a smooth elastic dough forms. Gather together in a ball and leave at room temperature for 2 hours. Cover with plastic wrap and refrigerate overnight, or for up to 3 days before using.

To mix the croissant dough by hand, put the flour, milk, sugar, ferment, salt and yeast in a bowl and use one hand to squeeze everything together until the mixture starts to resemble a crumbly dough. Turn out onto a clean work surface and knead for about 10–15 minutes.

If you are using an electric mixer, put the flour, milk, sugar, ferment, salt and yeast in the bowl of the mixer fitted with a dough hook. Process on low speed for about 3-4 minutes, then increase the speed to high and mix together for another 2 minutes.

You should have a smooth elastic dough that doesn't break when stretched gently. Gather the dough into a ball. Place in a plastic bag and refrigerate for at least 2 hours, or preferably overnight.

Before laminating, or folding, the pastry, remove the extra butter from the refrigerator — it should be cold but malleable. Use a rolling pin to gently pound the butter between sheets of baking paper into a 20 cm (8 inch) flat square about 1 cm (½ inch) thick.

Using a lightly floured rolling pin, roll the dough out into a rectangle, about 20 x 40 cm (8 x 16 inches). Place the butter in the centre of the dough and fold the dough over the top squeezing the edges together to completely enclose the butter. Carefully roll the dough out into a rectangle, about 20 x 90 cm (8 x 35½ inches). Fold the rectangle from one long end by one-third, so the dough is now 20 x 60 cm (8 x 24 inches). Fold the other long end over the top so that the dough is now 20 x 30 cm (8 x 12 inches). These folds are similar to the folding of a letter to place in an envelope.

Put the dough in a plastic bag or cover well with plastic wrap and refrigerate for about 20 minutes to allow the gluten to relax. Repeat this folding and resting process twice more, each time rotating the dough 90 degrees so that as you roll it out you are stretching it in the opposite direction to the previous fold.

Once the dough has been rolled and folded three times and had a final rest in the refrigerator for about 20 minutes, it is ready to be pinned out and shaped into croissants or used to make pan au raisin, pan au chocolat, danishes, bear claws or praline twists.

ingredients

300 g (10½ oz) unsalted butter, chilled, cut into 1.5 cm (⅝ inch) cubes

600 g (1 lb 5 oz/4 cups) plain (all-purpose) flour, chilled

5 g (⅛ oz/1 teaspoon) salt

15 ml (½ fl oz/3 teaspoons) vinegar, chilled

170 ml (5½ fl oz/⅔ cup) water, chilled

If you only ever want to make one pastry dough, then this is the one to make as it can be used to make both sweet and savoury products. Until working at Bourke Street Bakery this is the pastry I used for everything — sweet or savoury. The method for this recipe is very similar to sweet shortcrust pastry, so you can refer to the pictures on pages 156–7 to see a step-by-step breakdown of techniques.

This recipe makes enough pastry to make twelve 12.5 cm (4¾ inch) pies or quiches. If you are making any of the savoury pies you will only use half this amount, but rather than halve the quantity of the pastry we suggest you line all twelve shells and freeze six of them for future use. The pastry can be frozen for up to 2 months.

savoury shortcrust pastry
makes 1 quantity

method

Remove the butter from the refrigerator 20 minutes before you start mixing — the butter should be just soft but still very cold so it doesn't melt through the pastry while still mixing.

If you are mixing the dough by hand, mix together the flour and salt in a large bowl and toss through the butter. Use your fingertips to rub the butter into the flour to partly combine. If you are using a food processor, put the flour and salt in the bowl of the food processor and add the butter, pulsing in 1-second bursts about three or four times to partly combine.

You should now have a floury mix through which you can see squashed pieces of butter. Turn out onto a clean surface and gather together. Combine the vinegar with the chilled water and sprinkle it over the flour mixture. Use the palm of your hand to smear this mixture away from you across the bench. Gather together again and repeat this smearing process twice more before gathering the dough again. You may need to smear once or twice more to bring it together — you should still be able to see streaks of butter marbled through the pastry; this gives a slightly flaky texture to the final product. Divide into two even-sized portions and shape into two round, flat discs about 2 cm (¾ inch) thick. Wrap each disc in plastic wrap and refrigerate for at leat 2 hours or overnight.

Remove the pastry from the refrigerator 20 minutes before you wish to roll it. Sprinkle a little flour on the work surface and rub a little flour over your rolling pin. Working from the centre of the pastry, gently roll the pastry away from you, then turn the pastry about 30 degrees and roll out again. Continue to repeat this process until you have a flat round disc, about 3 mm (⅛ inch) thick. Sprinkle extra flour over the bench and rolling pin as needed, but try to use it as sparingly as possible — if too much is absorbed into the pastry as you roll it, unmixed flour will be added resulting in unappealing pastry that has a poor flavour and texture. As you are rolling the pastry, bear in mind that you are trying to flatten it into a disc, not ferociously stretch it out in all directions. Stretching will only cause the pastry to shrink excessively when baking. Return the pastry to the refrigerator, covered in plastic wrap, for at least 2 hours to allow the gluten to relax.

If you are using the pastry to make pies, brush twelve 12.5 cm (4¾ inch) pie tins with a little butter. Cut the pastry using a round pastry cutter with a 15 cm (6 inch) diameter. Place the dough on top of the mould ensuring it is in the centre and use your fingers to gently push the pastry into the mould, moving around the rim until all of the pastry has been inserted — you should now have about 1 cm (½ inch) of dough hanging over the sides. Gently fold this pastry over the tins to leave a wide rim for attaching the lid. Any pie cases that aren't going to be filled immediately can be frozen for up to 2 months.

ingredients

400 g (14 oz) unsalted butter, chilled, cut into
1.5 cm (⅝ inch) cubes
20 ml (½ fl oz/1 tablespoon) vinegar, chilled
100 g (3½ oz) caster (superfine) sugar, chilled
170 ml (5½ fl oz/⅔ cup) water, chilled
665 g (1 lb 7½ oz) plain (all-purpose) flour, chilled
5 g (⅛ oz/1 teaspoon) salt

sweet shortcrust pastry (pâté brisée)
makes 1 quantity

The following recipe for sweet shortcrust pastry will leave you with a slightly uneven edge around the rim of the tin when you line it. resulting in a tart that looks rustic and home-made. which is what we aim for at Bourke Street Bakery. If you are looking for a perfectly even effect. this is not the correct recipe to use. The fact that this dough has water in it means it will shrink as the water evaporates during baking: the following method is to help counteract this shrinkage. If you are looking for a perfect result. use the Sweet Pastry (Pâté Sablée) recipe on page 159. but keep in mind that it is a far more fragile dough than this one.

This recipe makes enough pastry for twenty 8 cm (3¼ inch) tarts with a little left-over. The number of tarts is going to vary from baker to baker depending on how thin the pastry is rolled. The pastry can be frozen for up to 2 months. so it makes sense to line all the shells. freeze them and simply blind bake them as you need them.

method

Remove the butter from the refrigerator 20 minutes before you start mixing — the butter should be just soft but still very cold so it doesn't melt through the pastry while mixing.

Put the vinegar and sugar in a bowl and add the water, stirring well. Set aside for 10 minutes, then stir again to completely dissolve the sugar.

If you are mixing the dough by hand, mix together the flour and salt in a large bowl and toss through the butter. Use your fingertips to rub the butter into the flour to partly combine.

If you are using a food processor, put the flour and salt in the bowl of the food processor and add the butter, pulsing in 1-second bursts about three or four times to partly combine

You should now have a floury mix through which you can see squashed pieces of butter. Turn out onto a clean work surface and gather together. Sprinkle over the sugar mixture and use the palm of your hand to smear this mixture away from you across the work surface (a pastry scraper is a useful tool to use for this step). Gather together again and repeat this smearing process twice more before gathering the dough again. You may need to smear once or twice more to bring it together — you should still be able to see streaks of butter marbled through the pastry; this gives a slightly flaky texture to the final product. Divide the dough into two even-sized portions and shape into two round, flat discs about 2 cm (¾ inch) thick. Wrap each disc in plastic wrap and refrigerate for at least 2 hours or overnight.

Remove the pastry from the refrigerator 20 minutes before you wish to roll it. Sprinkle a little flour on the bench and rub a little flour over a rolling pin. Working from the centre of the pastry, gently roll the dough away from you, then turn the dough about 30 degrees and roll out again. Repeat this process until you have a flat round disc, about 3 mm (⅛ inch) thick. Sprinkle extra flour over the bench and rolling pin as needed, but try to use it as sparingly as possible — if too much is absorbed into the pastry it will result in a dough with poor flavour and texture. Bear in mind that you are trying to flatten the pastry into a disc, not ferociously stretch it out in all directions. Stretching will only cause the pastry to shrink excessively when baking. Transfer the pastry to a tray and place in the refrigerator, covered in plastic wrap, for at least 2 hours to allow the gluten to relax.

At Bourke Street Bakery, we prefer to use loose-based tart tins and moulds, which have sides that are at an angle of about 90 degrees to the base. The right angle offers more support than sloping sides and makes it easier to remove a fragile tart. Again, it is important not to stretch the dough when lining the tins.

Brush twenty 8 cm (3¼ inch) individual tart tins with a little butter. Cut the pastry using a round pastry cutter with an 11 cm (4¼ inch) diameter. Place the pastry on top of the mould ensuring it is in the centre and use your fingers to gently push the pastry into the mould, moving around the rim until all of the pastry has been inserted — you should now have about 1 cm (½ inch) of dough hanging over the sides. Use your index finger and thumb to work your way around the edge, forcing the pastry into the mould so that little or no pastry is left protruding. Where the upright edge of the pastry meets the base there should be a sharp angle where it has been firmly forced into the corner — this method of lining the tin is to counteract the pastry shrinking once baked. Set the pastry cases aside to rest for at least 20 minutes in the freezer so that the gluten relaxes and holds its shape when you line it with foil.

Once the tart has been lined and rested, most recipes will call for it to be blind baked. Blind baking pastry simply means you need to pre-bake the pastry before filling it, to ensure the base is crisp and cooked through. If you own a pizza stone this will work perfectly, as long as it is heated well and the pastry tin is placed directly on the stone.

Preheat the oven to 200°C (400°F/Gas 6). Line the pastry with a double layer of aluminium foil, making sure the foil is pushed well into the corners. Pour in some baking beads or uncooked rice to fill the case and bake for 20–25 minutes — the baking time will vary considerably from oven to oven. When cooked properly, the pastry should have a golden colour all over, particularly in the centre, which tends to be the last part to colour and become crisp. The tart shells are now ready to be filled.

1. You can mix the dough by hand or with an electric mixer. Use your fingertips to rub the butter into the flour to partly combine.

2. Sprinkle over the sugar mixture and use the palm of your hand to smear the mixture away from you across the work surface.

5. Once the dough has rested for at least two hours use a round pastry cutter to cut out twenty circles, each with an 11 cm (4¼ inch) diameter.

6. To line the tins, place a pastry circle over each tin and press into the base. Moving around the rim, use your fingers to push the pastry into the tins.

3. Divide the dough into two even-sized discs, cover with plastic wrap and refrigerate for 2 hours.

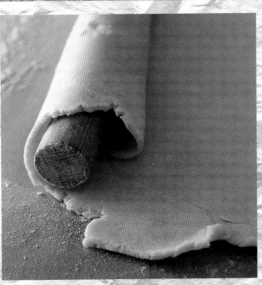

4. Roll out each disc to 3 mm (1/8 inch) thick, working from the centre of the dough and turning regularly. Use the rolling pin to lift the pastry onto a tray and refrigerate.

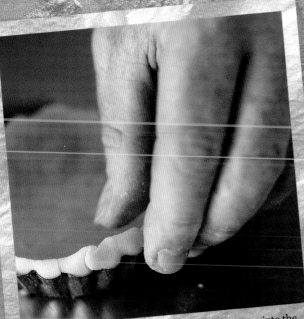

7. Use your index finger and thumb to force the pastry into the tin so that none is overhanging — there should be a sharp angle in the corner where the upright pastry meets the base.

8. Once the pastry is in the tins you can line the tins ready for blind baking. You can then freeze them for later use or blind bake them as needed.

ingredients

500 g (1 lb 2 oz) unsalted butter, chilled, cut into 1.5 cm (⅝ inch) cubes

10 g (¼ oz/2 teaspoons) salt

260 g (9¼ oz) icing (confectioners') sugar, sifted and chilled

80 g (2¾ oz/about 5) egg yolks, chilled

665 g (1 lb 7½ oz) plain (all-purpose) flour, chilled

This is a shorter pastry than the pâté brisée, meaning that it has a higher ratio of butter to flour. The fact that it has no water means that the texture of the pastry itself is more crumbly — it holds its shape better and remains crisper for longer than pâté brisée. You can use this as you would a shortcrust pastry.

sweet pastry (pâté sablée)

makes 1 quantity

method

Remove the butter from the refrigerator 20 minutes before you start mixing — the butter should be just soft but still very cold.

If you are mixing the dough by hand, put the butter, icing sugar and salt in a bowl and mix well with a wooden spoon to combine. Beat the yolks into the bowl, a little at a time, being sure it is completely combined before adding more. Use a wooden spoon to fold through the flour until just combined.

If you are using a food processor, put the butter, icing sugar and salt in the bowl of the food processor and pulse in 2-second bursts about ten times until the mixture is pale and creamy. Add the yolks, in two batches, pulsing for 2 seconds after each addition or until fully combined. Add the flour, in three batches, pulsing for 2 seconds after each addition.

Turn out onto a clean work surface and gather together. Divide into three even-sized portions and shape into round, flat discs about 2 cm (¾ inch) thick. Wrap each disc in plastic wrap and refrigerate for at least 2 hours or overnight.

Remove the pastry from the refrigerator 20 minutes before you wish to roll it. Roll out the pastry between sheets of baking paper until 2–3 cm (¾–1¼ inches) thick. Place on trays and refrigerate for 2 hours. Brush twenty 6.5 cm (2⅔ inch) individual tart tins with a little butter. Cut the pastry using a round pastry cutter with an 8.5 cm (3⅓ inch) diameter and use a 7 cm (2¾ inch) cutter for the lids. Re-roll to make use of all the dough. Follow the instructions for sweet shortcrust pastry on pages 154–7 to line the tins and proceed to fill the tarts as required.

ingredients

450 g (1 lb/3 cups) plain (all-purpose) flour

7 g (¼ oz/1½ teaspoons) salt

210 ml (7½ fl oz) water, chilled

1 teaspoon vinegar

1 egg

50 g (1¾ oz) suet (see note)

During the bakery's first summer, we shut up shop for five weeks and fled Surry Hills. Dave went to France and I went to South America. I fell in love with the empanadas. I ate so many my veins coursed with suet. Inspired on my return, I created the Bourke Street Empanada — not glamorous, not good for you — but damn tasty. An empanada for me is street food. It tastes so much better when eaten on the side of a lively road while watching the world go by — a perfect match for our little bakery.

You can make empanadas using puff or filo pastry instead of the empanada pastry below, and adjust the size of them depending on your personal taste or the occasion.

empanada dough   makes 1 quantity

method

To make the empanada dough put the flour and salt in a bowl. Make a well in the centre and add the water, vinegar and egg. Grate the suet into the middle and mix with a spoon until well incorporated and combined.

Turn the mixture out onto a lightly floured work surface and knead for 3 minutes, then set aside for 5 minutes so the dough can rest. Knead for a further 5 minutes, or until the dough is smooth and elastic. Cover in plastic wrap and refrigerate for 2 hours.

Roll out the dough to a 30 x 75 cm (12 x 29¼ inch) rectangle, about 2 mm (1/16 inch) thick. Using a pastry cutter or a similar round plate or lid, cut ten circles from the pastry with a 14 cm (5½ inch) diameter. Re-roll the offcuts and cut another two circles to make 12 circles in total. The empanada dough is now ready for filling (see pages 242–3).

note

Suet is hardened beef or mutton fat from around the loins and kidneys. It is available from speciality butchers.

ingredients

135 g (4¾ oz) unsalted butter, cut into 1.5 cm (⅝ inch) cubes, chilled
675 g (1 lb 8 oz/4½ cups) plain (all-purpose) flour, chilled
20 g (¾ oz/1 tablespoon) salt
20 ml (½ fl oz/1 tablespoon) vinegar, chilled
300 ml (10½ fl oz) water, chilled
500 g (1 lb 2 oz) unsalted butter, extra, for laminating, chilled

The thing that makes puff pastry unique is the way it is folded, known as laminating. Like croissants the dough is folded around the butter numerous times, creating layers, which result in a flakier pastry. It is perfect for making both savoury and sweet products — at the bakery we use it mostly for sausage rolls, pie lids and galettes. If you want to use puff pastry for a product you will need to start making it a day or two in advance.

puff pastry makes 1 quantity

method

Remove the cubed butter from the refrigerator 20 minutes before you start mixing — the butter should be just soft but still very cold so it doesn't melt through the pastry while still mixing.

If you are mixing the pastry by hand, mix together the flour and salt in a large bowl and toss through the butter. Use your fingertips to rub the butter into the flour to partly combine. Turn out onto a clean work surface and gather together. Combine the vinegar with the chilled water and sprinkle over the flour mixture. Knead gently to form a smooth dough.

If you are using a food processor, put the butter, flour and salt into the bowl of the food processor and pulse on high for about 30 seconds, or until the mixture resembles sand. Combine the vinegar with the chilled water and add to the bowl, pulsing in 3–4 bursts until you have a smooth dough.

Flatten the pastry into a round, flat disc about 2 cm (¾ inch) thick. Wrap in plastic wrap and refrigerate for at least 20 minutes or overnight.

Before laminating, or folding, the pastry, remove the extra butter from the refrigerator — it should be cold but malleable. Use a rolling pin to gently pound the butter between sheets of baking paper into a 20 cm (8 inch) flat square about 1 cm (½ inch) thick.

Remove the pastry from the refrigerator and roll it out on a lightly floured work surface to make a 20 x 40 cm (8 x 16 inch) rectangle. Place the butter at one end of the pastry and fold the other end over to completely enclose the butter.

Turn the pastry 90 degrees and begin to roll it away from you in even strokes. When you have a 20 x 90 cm (8 x 35½ inch) rectangle, fold in both ends to meet in the middle. Fold the pastry in half again to close it, as if you were closing a book — look at the pastry and visualise the spine of the book on one side and the pages on the other. Dust the pastry lightly with flour, cover, and refrigerate for 30 minutes. This completes the first fold.

Repeat this folding process three more times to make four folds in total. Each time you roll the pastry, place it on the bench with the 'book spine' edge running at 90 degrees to the front of the bench on the left-hand side; this will ensure you are rotating the pastry 90 degrees each time you roll and fold it. Refrigerate the pastry for 30 minutes between each fold to allow the gluten to relax, otherwise it will be hard to roll and the pastry will be more likely to shrink when baked. Some chefs prefer to make the first two folds then rest the pastry overnight in the refrigerator, doing the final two folds 24 hours later. This method results in more defined layers and is preferable if time and refrigerator space permits. If you use this method, be sure to allow the pastry to sit out of the refrigerator for about 30 minutes after the overnight period to allow it to become malleable again. After the laminating is complete, a 24-hour rest in the refrigerator is again preferable to stop shrinkage. After this time, the dough is best used within 1 day or frozen, as it discolours very quickly.

Remove the pastry from the refrigerator 30 minutes before you wish to roll it. Sprinkle a little flour on the bench and over the rolling pin. Working from the centre of the pastry, gently roll it away from you, then turn the pastry about 45 degrees and roll out again. Repeat this process until you have a flat rectangular or square disc about 5 mm (¼ inch) thick.

Refrigerate the pastry for at least 30 minutes before cutting into the desired shapes. When cutting, drag a sharp knife across the pastry rather than using a downward action — this stops the edge of the pastry becoming crushed, which would result in poor rising and loss of all the beautiful layers you have spent hours folding into the pastry.

If you are making pie lids, use a round pastry cutter to cut out circles for them, making sure they have a diameter that is at least 1 cm (½ inch) larger than the base of the tin, so that you can easily attach them and seal.

note

Any unused pastry can be rolled out, cut into the desired shapes and stored in the freezer for up to 2 months, covered in plastic wrap. Bake directly from the freezer.

1. Once you have mixed and rested the pastry you can start laminating. First you need to roll the pastry out into a rectangle, about 20 x 40 cm (8 x 16 inches).

2. When the butter has been pounded into shape, place it at one end of the pastry and fold over the other end to cover.

5. Once you have the desired length, fold the two short ends over to meet in the middle.

6. The pastry is then folded in half again, as if you were closing a book.

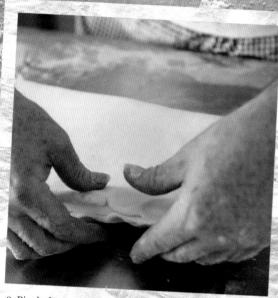

3. Pinch the pastry around the exposed butter to completely enclose it inside the pastry.

4. Turn the dough 90 degrees and roll it out using even strokes to create a 20 x 90 cm (8 x 35 1/2 inch) long rectangle.

7. The pastry needs to be dusted lightly with flour, covered with plastic wrap and then refrigerated for 30 minutes — this completes the first fold.

8. Repeat this folding process three more times, turning the pastry 90 degrees each time. Once the laminating is complete, refrigerate the pastry for 24 hours before using.

croissants and danishes

At the Bakery, we believe that the reason people have been known to queue up outside the door in the mornings is not just for a great cup of coffee, but to experience the theatre of watching freshly baked pastries as they are pulled from the oven.

Morning pastries are based on the croissant and Danish doughs and are known as the viennoiserie section in the French kitchen. They are some of the most difficult to master, but once you get enough practice they soon become second nature. By following a few of these basic rules you will quickly be rewarded with excellent results.

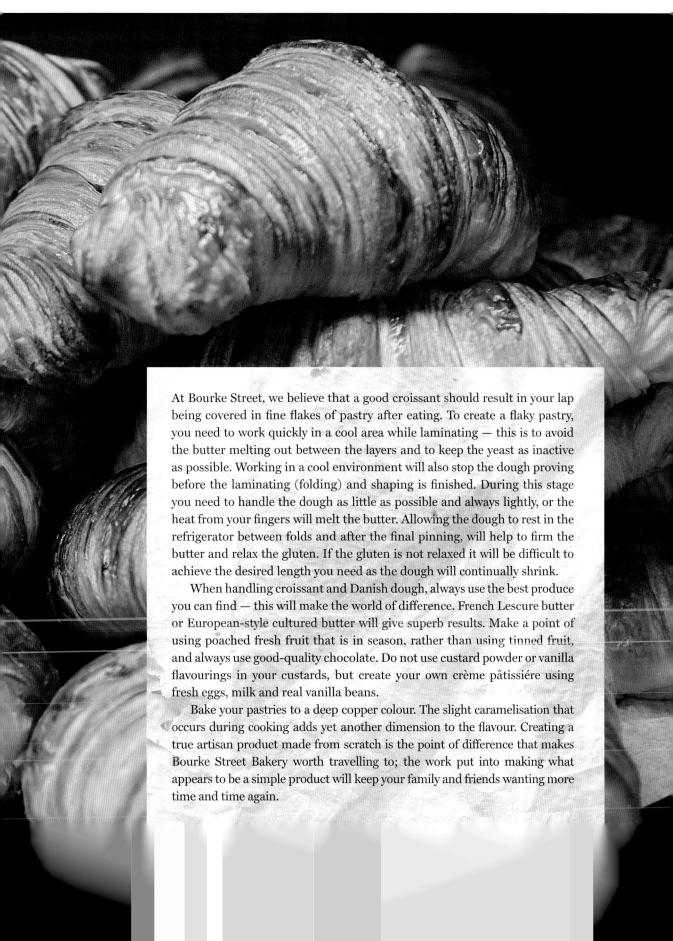

At Bourke Street, we believe that a good croissant should result in your lap being covered in fine flakes of pastry after eating. To create a flaky pastry, you need to work quickly in a cool area while laminating — this is to avoid the butter melting out between the layers and to keep the yeast as inactive as possible. Working in a cool environment will also stop the dough proving before the laminating (folding) and shaping is finished. During this stage you need to handle the dough as little as possible and always lightly, or the heat from your fingers will melt the butter. Allowing the dough to rest in the refrigerator between folds and after the final pinning, will help to firm the butter and relax the gluten. If the gluten is not relaxed it will be difficult to achieve the desired length you need as the dough will continually shrink.

When handling croissant and Danish dough, always use the best produce you can find — this will make the world of difference. French Lescure butter or European-style cultured butter will give superb results. Make a point of using poached fresh fruit that is in season, rather than using tinned fruit, and always use good-quality chocolate. Do not use custard powder or vanilla flavourings in your custards, but create your own crème pâtissiére using fresh eggs, milk and real vanilla beans.

Bake your pastries to a deep copper colour. The slight caramelisation that occurs during cooking adds yet another dimension to the flavour. Creating a true artisan product made from scratch is the point of difference that makes Bourke Street Bakery worth travelling to; the work put into making what appears to be a simple product will keep your family and friends wanting more time and time again.

ingredients

egg wash

1 egg

100 ml (3½ fl oz) milk

a pinch of salt

1 quantity croissant dough (see pages 148–9)

croissants

makes 18

method

To make the egg wash, put the egg, milk and salt in a bowl and whisk with a fork until well combined. Set aside until needed.

Take the rested dough from the refrigerator and roll it out into a rectangle, about 25 x 100 cm (10 x 39½ inches) and about 5–8 mm (¼–⅜ inch) thick. Rolling the dough may take quite a lot of energy as it may keep springing back to its original size. If this happens, rest the dough in the refrigerator for about 10 minutes then resume rolling. This resting process may need to be done a number of times. If the dough is becoming too large to fit in the refrigerator simply fold it over and place on a tray before placing it in.

Cut the rolled dough into 18 triangles with a base that is 9 cm (3½ inches) wide and two sides that are 21 cm (8¼ inches) high — you may wish to prepare a template by drawing the dimensions on a piece of cardboard and cutting out a triangle to use as a guide.

Stack the triangles on a tray lined with baking paper, cover lightly with a clean tea towel (dish towel) and place in the refrigerator for about 10 minutes. Remove from the refrigerator and, working with one triangle at a time, gently stretch it out slightly. Starting from the base end roll up towards the tip, pressing the tip to secure (see pictures, page 170).

Preheat the oven to 240°C (475°F/Gas 8). Place the rolled croissants back onto the lined trays at well-spaced intervals. Cover loosely with a damp tea towel. Set aside in a warm room (about 25°C–27°C/77°F–81°F) for 1½–2 hours, or until almost doubled in size. Spray the tea towel with water occasionally if it becomes dry.

Remove the tea towel, brush the top of each croissant lightly with egg wash and place in the oven. Reduce the oven temperature to 190°C (375°F/Gas 5) and bake for about 15 minutes, or until a deep golden colour. Cool slightly on the trays before serving.

1. Once you have cut out the triangles, start from the base end and roll up towards the tip. Use an even pressure as you roll and press the tip to secure once rolled.

2. Repeat this rolling process until all the pastry is used and set aside for 1½-2 hours until doubled in size.

ingredients

1 quantity croissant dough (see pages 148–9)

480 g (1 lb 1 oz) dark chocolate (55% cocoa), roughly chopped

egg wash (see page 168), for brushing

If you are a chocolate lover, this is the morning pastry for you – basically it is a croissant wrapped around the best-quality chocolate you can find. At the bakery we use chocolate sticks that have been specially created for this purpose, which are available from speciality providores.

pan au chocolat makes 24

method

Take the rested dough from the refrigerator and roll it out into a rectangle, about 35 x 100 cm (14 x 39½ inches) and about 5 mm (¼ inch) thick. Rolling the dough may take quite a lot of energy as it may keep springing back to its original size. If this happens, rest the dough in the refrigerator for about 10 minutes then resume rolling. This resting process may need to be done a number of times. If the dough is becoming too large to fit in the refrigerator simply fold it over and place on a tray before placing it in.

Cut the dough into 24 rectangles, about 8 x 16 cm (3¼ x 6¼ inch) each. Place the rectangles on trays lined with baking paper and place in the refrigerator for 10 minutes. Remove from the refrigerator. Using 10 g (¼ oz) of the chocolate, place a line of the chopped pieces at the narrow end closest to you and fold the dough over to enclose. Using another 10 g (¼ oz) chocolate, place another line to sit beside the first and continue rolling the dough to form a log (see pictures, page 174). Repeat with the remaining pastry pieces and chocolate.

Preheat the oven to 240°C (475°F/Gas 8). Place the pan au chocolat back onto the lined trays at well-spaced intervals, seam side down. Cover loosely with a damp tea towel (dish towel). Set aside in a warm room (about 25°C–27°C/77°F–81°F) for 1½–2 hours, or until almost doubled in size. Spray the tea towel with water occasionally if it becomes dry.

Remove the tea towel, brush the top of each pan au chocolat lightly with egg wash and place in the oven. Reduce the oven temperature to 190°C (375°F/Gas 5) and bake for about 15 minutes, or until a deep golden colour. Cool slightly on the trays before serving.

1. Place a line of chocolate pieces or a chocolate stick at one end of each pastry rectangle and fold the pastry over to enclose.

2. Place another line of chocolate pieces or a chocolate stick directly next to the first and firmly roll over to enclose.

3. Roll up the rest of the pastry to form a log shape, press down to close the seam and place on baking trays lined with baking paper.

4. Once all the logs are rolled, cover with a damp tea towel (dish towel) and set aside for 1½–2 hours until doubled in size, before baking.

ingredients

600 g (1 lb 5 oz/4$\frac{3}{4}$ cup) sultanas (golden raisins)

200 g (7 oz/1$\frac{1}{3}$ cups) currants

1.25 litres (44 fl oz/5 cups) boiling water

60 g (2$\frac{1}{4}$ oz/1$\frac{1}{3}$ cup) soft brown sugar

$\frac{1}{2}$ teaspoon mixed (pumpkin pie) spice

1 quantity croissant dough (see pages 148–9)

250 g (9 oz/1 cup) crème pâtissiére (see pages 276–7)

egg wash (see page 168), for brushing

icing (confectioners') sugar, for dusting

Most kids growing up in Australia will know these as snails, a name they were given due to the shape of the pastry, which is folded into a spiral shape. You will need to make the fruit mix and crème pâtissiére at least one day in advance.

pan au raisin
makes 30

method

To make the fruit mix, put the sultanas and currants in a mixing bowl. Pour over the boiling water and set aside to cool. Cover with plastic wrap and place in the refrigerator overnight, or for up to 2–3 days. Drain the fruit and add the brown sugar and mixed spice, stirring well to combine. Set aside.

Take the rested dough from the refrigerator and roll it out into a rectangle, about 35 x 100 cm (14 x 39$\frac{1}{2}$ inches) and about 5 mm ($\frac{1}{4}$ inch) thick. Rolling the dough may take quite a lot of energy as it may keep springing back to its original size. If this happens, rest the dough in the refrigerator for about 10 minutes then resume rolling. This resting process may need to be done a number of times. If the dough is becoming too large to fit in the refrigerator simply fold it over and place on a tray before placing it in.

Cut the dough in half to make two 35 x 50 cm (14 x 20 inch) rectangles. Place the dough on trays lined with baking paper and place in the refrigerator for about 10 minutes.

Lay one sheet of dough on a lightly floured surface, with the short length running parallel to the edge of the bench. Spread $\frac{1}{2}$ cup of crème pâtissiére evenly over the rectangle, spreading all the way to the edges. Top the rectangle with half of the fruit mix to evenly cover the crème pâtissiére. Starting with the short edge furthest away from you, firmly and tightly roll the dough towards you, as if rolling a newspaper for delivery. Wrap the log in baking paper and place in the refrigerator for about 20 minutes to firm up. Repeat with the remaining sheet of dough.

Remove the baking paper from both logs and place the dough on a clean work surface. Cut each log into slices, about 1.5 cm (⅝ inch) wide, to make about 30 rounds in total.

Preheat the oven to 240°C (475°F/Gas 8). Place the rolls back onto the lined trays at well-spaced intervals. Cover loosely with a damp tea towel (dish towel). Set aside in a warm room (about 25°C–27°C/77°F– 81°F) for 1½–2 hours, or until almost doubled in size. Spray the tea towel with water occasionally if it becomes dry.

Remove the tea towel, brush the top of each pan au raisin lightly with egg wash and place in the oven. Reduce the oven temperature to 190°C (375°F/Gas 5) and bake for about 15 minutes, or until a deep golden colour. Cool slightly on the trays before dusting with icing sugar and serving.

400 g (14 oz/1¾ cups) caster (superfine) sugar

40 ml (1¼ fl oz) liquid glucose

200 ml (7 fl oz) water

200 g (7 oz) blanched almonds

1 quantity croissant dough (see pages 148–9)

250 g (9 oz/1 cup) crème pâtissiére (see page 276–7)

egg wash (see page 168), for brushing

icing (confectioners') sugar, for dusting

This is one of our most popular croissants. The soft, sticky dough with the crunch of the nuts and toffee is a real winner with customers dropping by for their morning coffee. It's a favourite with the bakers too, but they love a part of the twist the customers don't see, it's the buttery caramel that oozes out during baking and forms a paper thin crust on the baking paper.

praline twists makes 60

method

To make the praline, put the sugar and liquid glucose in a saucepan over medium heat. Add the water and bring to the boil, stirring well to dissolve the sugar. As a rule, when mixing high ratios of sugar into water, once the water boils the stirring stops to prevent the sugar from crystallising. Instead of stirring, keep a pastry brush in a small bowl of water on hand and brush down the insides of the saucepan to stop any sugar crystals forming. Keep boiling the mixture until it is a deep caramel colour.

Remove from the heat and add the almonds; the mixture will be hot so take care not to splash yourself. Pour the mixture into a deep baking tray lined with baking paper. Set aside to cool then, using a meat mallet or similar heavy object, break the nut caramel into rough 3 cm (1¼ inch) pieces. Put in a food processor and process until the mixture resembles coarse breadcrumbs. Set aside until needed.

Take the rested dough from the refrigerator and roll it out into a rectangle, about 35 x 100 cm (14 x 39½ inches) and about 5 mm (¼ inch) thick. Rolling the dough may take quite a lot of energy as it may keep springing back to its original size. If this happens, rest the dough in the refrigerator for about 10 minutes then resume rolling. This resting process may need to be done a number of times. If the dough is becoming too large to fit in the refrigerator simply fold it over and place on a tray before placing it in.

Cut the dough in half to make two 35 x 50 cm (14 x 20 inch) rectangles. Place the dough on trays lined with baking paper and place in the refrigerator for about 10 minutes.

Lay one sheet of dough on a lightly floured surface, with the short length running parallel to the edge of the bench. Spread ½ cup of crème pâtissiére evenly over the rectangle, spreading all the way to the edges. Top the rectangle with one-quarter of the praline to evenly cover the crème pâtissiére. Starting with the short edge furthest away from you, firmly and tightly roll the dough towards you, until you reach the centre of the dough. Then, starting from the side nearest to you, roll back to meet the first rolled half in the centre. Wrap the log in baking paper and place in the refrigerator for about 20 minutes to firm up. Repeat with the remaining sheet of dough.

Remove the baking paper and place the dough on a clean work surface. Cut each log into slices, about 1.5 cm (⅝ inch) wide. Pour the remaining praline onto the work surface. Twist the scroll shape so that the cross-section makes a figure eight and press both sides of each twist into the praline to coat evenly on both sides.

Preheat the oven to 240°C (475°F/Gas 8). Place the praline twists back onto the lined trays at well-spaced intervals. Cover loosely with a thin damp tea towel (dish towel). Set aside in a warm room (about 25°C–27°C/77°F–81°F) for 1½–2 hours, or until almost doubled in size. Spray the tea towel with water occasionally if it becomes dry.

Remove the tea towel, brush the top of each twist lightly with egg wash and place in the oven. Reduce the oven temperature to 190°C (375°F/Gas 5) and bake for about 15 minutes, or until a deep golden colour. Cool slightly on trays before dusting with icing sugar and serving.

ingredients

roasted rhubarb

2 kg (4 lb 8 oz) rhubarb, trimmed, rinsed
and cut into 3 cm (1¼ inch) pieces

850 g (1 lb 14 oz) vanilla sugar (see note)

1 quantity croissant dough (see pages 148–9)

250 g (9 oz/1 cup) crème pâtissiére (see page 276–7)

egg wash (see page 168), for brushing

This is a lovely way to cook rhubarb, intensifying its flavour and colour. In-season plums are the other fruit we regularly cook in this way: the sugar can be increased or decreased depending on the ripeness of the fruit and sweetness desired. The syrup that the fruit creates during cooking is used to cover the fruit when storing. The syrup can be used to make jelly, or you can simply serve the fruit and syrup with ice cream for a quick dessert. You will need to prepare the rhubarb and crème pâtissiére a day in advance.

rhubarb danishes makes 36

method

To make the roasted rhubarb, preheat the oven to 160°C (315°F/Gas 2–3). Place the rhubarb in two baking trays so that it fits snugly and sprinkle over the vanilla sugar. Cover loosely with foil and bake for about 12–15 minutes, checking every 5 minutes, until the rhubarb pieces are just soft but still holding their shape. Remove from the oven, allow to cool, and store in the syrup in an airtight container. Refrigerate until needed.

Take the rested dough from the refrigerator and roll it out into a rectangle, about 40 x 85 cm (16 x 33½ inches) and about 5 mm (¼ inch) thick. Rolling the dough may take quite a lot of energy as it may keep springing back to its original size. If this happens, rest the dough in the refrigerator for about 10 minutes then resume rolling. This resting process may need to be done a number of times. If the dough is becoming too large for the refrigerator simply fold it over and place on a tray before placing it in.

Cut the dough into thirty-six 9 cm (3½ inch) squares. Place the squares on trays lined with baking paper and place in the refrigerator for about 10 minutes.

Remove the squares from the refrigerator and working with one square at a time, fold each corner to meet in the centre pressing down firmly to create a smaller square. Arrange the Danishes back on the lined trays at well-spaced intervals. Place 1½ teaspoons of crème pâtissiére in the centre of each Danish and top with about 5 pieces of rhubarb.

Preheat the oven to 240°C (475°F/Gas 8). Cover the Danishes loosely with a damp tea towel (dish towel). Set aside in a warm room (about 25°C–27°C/77°F–81°F) for 1½–2 hours, or until almost doubled in size. Spray the tea towel with water occasionally if it becomes dry.

Remove the tea towel, brush the top of each Danish lightly with egg wash and place in the oven. Reduce the oven temperature to 190°C (375°F/Gas 5) and bake for about 15 minutes, or until a deep golden colour. Cool slightly on trays before dusting with icing sugar and serving.

note

You can make your own vanilla sugar or buy it from most supermarkets. Making your own is preferable and is quite easy. It simply involves storing one vanilla bean per 500 g (1 lb 2 oz) of caster (superfine) sugar in an airtight container for at least 1 week; this will impart a wonderful aroma and is the best way to store vanilla beans before using to get double the use from them.

ingredients

poached pears

1 vanilla bean

1.2 kg (2 lb 10 oz/5¼ cups) caster (superfine) sugar

2 lemons, sliced

2 litres (70 fl oz/8 cups) water

10 Buerre bosc pears, peeled, cored and cut into eighths

1 quantity croissant dough (see page 148–9)

250 g (9 oz/1 cup) crème pâtissiére (see page 276–7)

egg wash (see page 168), for brushing

At Bourke Street Bakery we pretend this is the healthy alternative to the butter-laden croissant because of the addition of freshly poached fruit. It is possible to substitute other fruit for the pears in this Danish. Peaches are delicious when they're in season, as are plums. You may also wish to replace the vanilla with cinnamon sticks or a mix of star anise, cinnamon, cloves and a strip of orange peel. The sliced lemon is added to stop the fruit from discolouring. You will need to poach the pears and prepare the crème pâtissiére at least one day in advance.

pear danishes
makes 36

method

To make the poached pears, split the vanilla bean lengthways and scrape the seeds into a saucepan. Add the sugar, lemon and water. Bring to the boil over high heat, stirring well to dissolve the sugar, then reduce the heat to a very slow simmer. Add the pears to the simmering syrup and cook for about 20 minutes, or until they are easily pierced with a skewer — the poaching time will vary according to the ripeness of the fruit. Remove from the heat, allow to cool, and store in the syrup in an airtight container. Refrigerate until needed.

Take the rested dough from the refrigerator and roll it out into a rectangle, about 40 x 85 cm (16 x 33½ inches) and about 5 mm (¼ inch) thick. Rolling the dough may take quite a lot of energy as it may keep springing back to its original size. If this happens, rest the dough in the refrigerator for about 10 minutes then resume rolling. This resting process may need to be done a number of times. If the dough is becoming too large to fit in the refrigerator simply fold it over and place on a tray before placing it in.

Cut the dough into thirty-six 9 cm (3½ inch) squares. Place the squares on trays lined with baking paper and place in the refrigerator for about 10 minutes.

Remove the squares from the fridge and working with one square at a time, fold each corner to meet in the centre pressing down firmly to create a smaller square. Arrange the Danishes back onto the lined trays at well-spaced intervals. Place 1½ teaspoons of crème pâtissiére in the centre of each Danish and top with two pieces of pear.

Preheat the oven to 240°C (475°F/Gas 8). Cover the Danishes loosely with a damp tea towel (dish towel) and set aside in a warm room (about 25°C–27°C/77°F–81°F) for 1½–2 hours, or until almost doubled in size. Spray the tea towel with water occasionally if it becomes dry.

Remove the tea towel, brush the top of each Danish lightly with egg wash and place in the oven. Reduce the oven temperature to 190°C (375°F/Gas 5) and bake for about 15 minutes, or until a deep golden colour. Cool slightly on trays before dusting with icing sugar and serving.

625 g (1 lb 6 oz/2½ cups) frangipane (see page 276–7)

1 quantity croissant dough (see pages 148–9)

egg wash (see page 168), for brushing

icing (confectioners') sugar, for dusting

Eat the crunchy toes off the bear claws before reaching the soft frangipane centre of this delectable pastry. You can fill it with fruit if you wish or a mix of fruit and frangipane.

bear claws

makes 28

method

Take the rested dough from the refrigerator and roll it out into a rectangle, about 35 x 100 cm (14 x 39½ inches). This will take quite a lot of energy as the dough may keep springing back to its original size. If this happens rest the dough in the refrigerator for about 10 minutes then resume rolling. This resting process may need to be done a number of times. If the dough is becoming too large to fit in the refrigerator simply fold it over before placing on trays and placing it in.

Cut the dough into twenty-eight 8 x 14 cm (3¼ x 5½ inch) rectangles. Place the rectangles on trays lined with baking paper and place in the refrigerator for about 10 minutes.

Remove from the refrigerator and place 1 tablespoon of frangipane in the centre of each rectangle. Fold the dough in half lengthways, pressing the edges to seal. Make four 3 cm (1¼ inch) cuts on the wider sealed side to resemble the toes of a bear.

Preheat the oven to 240°C (475°F/Gas 8). Cover the bear claws loosely with a thin damp tea towel (dish towel). Set aside in a warm room (about 25°C–27°C/77°F–81°F) for 1½–2 hours, or until almost doubled in size. Spray the tea towel with water occasionally if it becomes dry.

Remove the tea towel, brush the top of each bear claw lightly with egg wash and place in the oven. Reduce the oven temperature to 190°C (375°F/Gas 5) and bake for about 15 minutes, or until a deep golden colour. Cool slightly on the trays before dusting with icing sugar and serving.

pies and sausage rolls

Without a doubt the pies and sausage rolls at Bourke Street Bakery have a special place in our hearts — we take them very seriously! A bad pie is just un-Australian.

To make a good pie you have to get a few things right. Firstly and most importantly, the filling should be saucy, without presenting a danger to your tie and shirt, and the meat should be tender and succulent. The next most important aspect is the pastry base. Providing all the structure, the savoury shortcrust pastry should be firm enough so that you can hold and eat the pie with one hand. The base should be no thicker than a few millimetres or it will impinge on the filling that is rightfully yours.

These days, most pies are made with pastry margarine, which acts as a solidifying agent to keep the base firm, but it also leaves you with a nasty film on the roof of your mouth. Butter is better. At Bourke Street we have been through a few shortcrust variations to find the perfect balancing act of butter and flour — the more butter you put in the recipe the limper the base will be. Lastly, we top our pies with puff pastry. Most bakeries just use the same pastry for the whole pie and no doubt that would be easier. But we found that another texture of pastry really enhances the whole pie-eating experience, especially when it is crisp flaky puff pastry that melts in your mouth.

An option for those who live in the fast lane and don't have the time to devote to making two pastries, is to make the filling and spoon it directly into a baking dish. Brush or spray the sides of the dish with olive oil, then top it with the pastry of your choice (usually puff pastry). Brush the pastry lid with egg wash and poke a whole in the centre of the lid to allow steam to escape. Pop it into a preheated 220°C (425°F/Gas 7) oven, reduce the temperature to 190°C (375°F/Gas 5) before cooking and bake for 30 minutes, or until golden brown.

And then there's the sausage roll. At Bourke Street we believe that the sausage roll has been overlooked for too long. Long, proud and full of meat, the sausage roll has somehow slipped into being less than it should be — less meat and more breadcrumbs. Growing up in Australia, one of the great cultural food debates in all walks of life was what actually went into sausage rolls and pies.

Sold by the school or sportsground canteen and supplied by large food corporations, sausage rolls lost the ability to be pure and tasty, which is hard to comprehend. Flavoured meat wrapped in puff pastry is not hard to make and is very moreish. We follow a few simple steps; we use quality meat from a premium butcher, fresh flavourings and great puff pastry. Rolling these savoury pastries by hand also helps.

ingredients

40 ml (1¼ fl oz/2 tablespoons) extra virgin olive oil

150 g (5½ oz) onions, peeled and cut into 1–1.5 cm (½–⅝ inch) cubes

3 garlic cloves, finely chopped

4 thyme sprigs, leaves picked

150 g (5½ oz) carrots, cut into 1–1.5 cm (½–⅝ inch) cubes

150 g (5½ oz) celery, cut into 1–1.5 cm (½–⅝ inch) cubes

375 g (13 oz) tomatoes, roughly chopped

55 ml (1¾ fl oz) malt vinegar

10 g (¼ oz/2 teaspoons) salt

2½ g (1/16 oz/1 teaspoon) white pepper

900 g (2 lb) cubed beef cheeks, trimmed of fat, cut into 2–3 cm (¾–1¼ inch) cubes

4 g (⅛ oz/1 teaspoon) potato flour

1 quantity savoury shortcrust pastry (see pages 150–1)

½ quantity puff pastry (see pages 162–5)

egg wash (see page 168), for brushing

humble beef pie

makes 6

We use beef cheek in this pie, which is the perfect cut of meat. It braises really well, holds its shape, has a beautiful, earthy, gelatinous meaty flavour and most importantly, it doesn't dry out like so many other braising cuts. Having said that, the beef cheek can be annoying to clean, so it is best to ask your butcher to do it for you, and then have it diced into 2–3 cm (¾ – 1¼ inch) cubes. For the best result, order an extra 100 g (3½ oz) of beef cheek so that you can trim all the sinew off, but be sure to check the final weight before adding to the filling.

method

Heat the oil in a saucepan over low heat and cook the onion, garlic and thyme for 5 minutes, or until softened. Add the carrot and celery and cook for 5 minutes. Add the tomato, vinegar, salt and pepper and simmer for a further 5 minutes, stirring to combine.

Add the beef to the pan and pour in enough water to cover the meat. Bring to the boil, reduce the heat and simmer for about 2 hours, skimming and stirring every 20 minutes or so, until the meat is just tender but still with texture. The beef should not be falling apart and the liquid should be noticeably thicker. Do not overcook the beef, as it will continue to cook when it cools down and will be cooked again when you bake the pie itself. If the beef cheek is poorly trimmed you may end up with pieces that are mostly gristle — these pieces should be spooned out of the mix and thrown away.

When the beef pieces are just tender, remove to a plate and set aside. Strain the cooking liquid and return to the warm pan over high heat. Continue cooking the liquid until reduced by about one-third. Mix together the potato flour and 2 teaspoons water and add to the cooking liquid, stirring well to combine. Return the beef to the liquid. Season with more salt and white pepper, to taste. Pour the mixture into a container with a large surface area, to cool the mix down as quickly as possible, stirring every now and again as it cools.

Preheat the oven to 200°C (400°F/Gas 6). Roll out the savoury pastry following the instructions on pages 150–1 and use it to line the base and sides of six 12.5 cm (4¾ inch) pie tins. Roll out the puff pastry following the instructions on pages 162–5 and cut out six circles with a 13.5 cm (5¼ inch) diameter to make the pie lids.

Spoon the mixture into the pastry-lined pie tins, filling them to the brim. To attach the puff pastry lids, brush the rim of the pastry base and lid with a little egg wash and lay the lid over the base. Pinch gently between your thumb and index finger to make a good seal around the circumference edge. Brush the top of the pie lid with egg wash and make a small hole in the middle to allow steam to escape. Reduce the oven temperature to 180°C (350°F/Gas 4) and bake the pies for 30–35 minutes, or until golden brown on top. Remove the pies from the tins and allow to cool for a few minutes before serving.

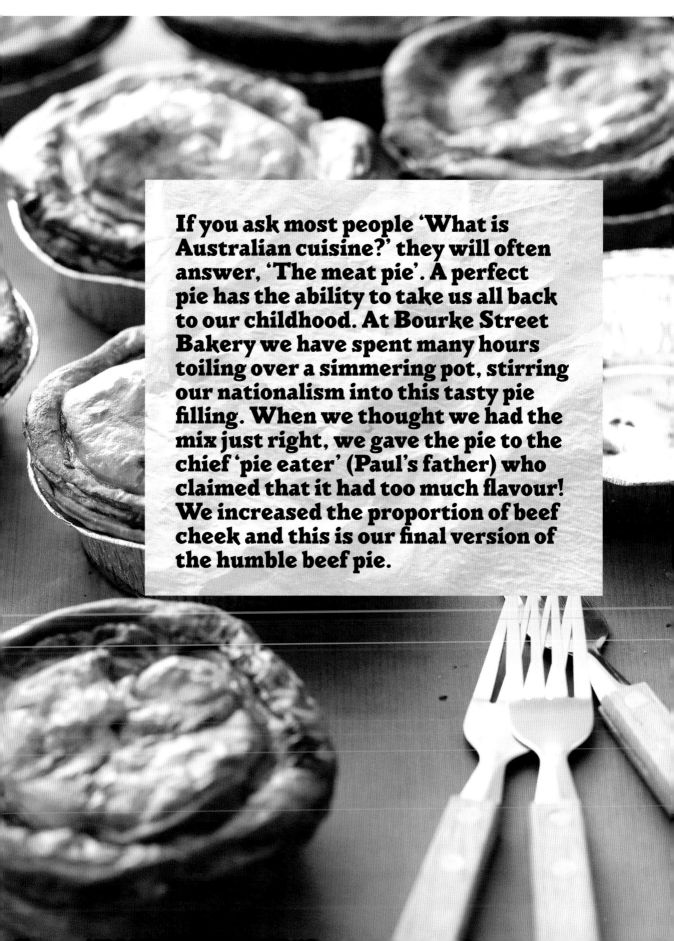

If you ask most people 'What is Australian cuisine?' they will often answer, 'The meat pie'. A perfect pie has the ability to take us all back to our childhood. At Bourke Street Bakery we have spent many hours toiling over a simmering pot, stirring our nationalism into this tasty pie filling. When we thought we had the mix just right, we gave the pie to the chief 'pie eater' (Paul's father) who claimed that it had too much flavour! We increased the proportion of beef cheek and this is our final version of the humble beef pie.

ingredients

250 g (9 oz) eggplant (aubergine), cut into 3 cm (1¼ inch) cubes

60 ml (2 fl oz/¼ cup) extra virgin olive oil

125 g (4½ oz) brown onions, finely chopped

4 garlic cloves, finely chopped

6 thyme sprigs, leaves picked

750 g (1 lb 10 oz) skinless, boneless chicken thigh fillets,
cut into 3 cm (1¼ inch) cubes

55 ml (1¾ fl oz) verjuice

250 g (9 oz) button mushrooms, quartered

5 g (⅛ oz/1 teaspoon) white pepper

5 g (⅛ oz/1 teaspoon) salt

50 g (1¾ oz) parmesan cheese, grated

1 handful basil, leaves torn

1 quantity savoury shortcrust pastry (see pages 150–1)

½ quantity puff pastry (see pages 162–5)

egg wash, for brushing (see page 168)

sesame seeds, for sprinkling

pepitas (pumpkin seeds), for sprinkling

béchamel sauce

125 ml (4 fl oz/½ cup) milk

12 g (⅓ oz) butter

12 g (⅓ oz) plain (all-purpose) flour, sifted

chicken pies with eggplant and mushroom

makes 6

This is a wonderfully simple chicken pie with big chunks of chicken, mushrooms, eggplant and whole basil leaves in a béchamel sauce. You should be able to taste each ingredient individually and the pie as a whole.

method

Preheat the oven to 220°C (425°F/Gas 7). Put the eggplant cubes in a single layer on a tray and sprinkle with a little salt. Set aside for 10 minutes, then rinse well. Put the eggplant on a baking tray lined with baking paper, drizzle with half of the olive oil and cook for about 15–20 minutes, or until tender. Remove from the oven and set aside.

Heat the remaining oil in a large saucepan over medium heat. Add the onion, garlic and thyme and cook for 5 minutes, or until softened. Add the chicken and cook for 5 minutes, stirring often. Add the verjuice and stir for about 30 seconds, or until reduced slightly, then pour in enough water to cover the chicken. Bring to the boil, then reduce the heat and simmer for 1 hour, or until the chicken is tender.

Add the mushrooms and baked eggplant to the pan and add the white pepper and salt. Cook for a further 10 minutes, or until the mushrooms have cooked through, then strain off the liquid into another saucepan, reserving the chicken mixture in a large container. Continue to cook the liquid over high heat, or until reduced by half.

To make the béchamel sauce, heat the milk in a saucepan over low heat so it is just slightly warm (not hot). Melt the butter in a separate saucepan and add the flour, stirring until the mixture catches on the edge of the pan. Slowly pour in the warm milk and whisk until smooth and thick. Remove from the heat and whisk into the vegetable mixture until smooth. Add the parmesan and stir to combine. Pour the sauce over the chicken mixture and stir through, then adjust the seasoning. Allow to cool before stirring through the torn basil leaves.

Roll out the savoury pastry following the instructions on pages 150–1 and use it to line the base and sides of six 12.5 cm (4¾ inch) pie tins. Roll out the puff pastry following the instructions on pages 162–5 and cut out six circles with a 13.5 cm (5¼ inch) diameter to make the pie lids.

Spoon the mixture into the pastry-lined pie tins, filling them to the brim. To attach the puff pastry lids, brush the rim of the pastry base and lid with a little egg wash and lay the lid over the base. Pinch gently between your thumb and index finger to make a good seal around the circumference edge. Brush the top of the pie lid with egg wash, sprinkle with sesame seeds and pepitas, and make a small hole in the middle to allow steam to escape. Reduce the oven temperature to 180°C (350°F/Gas 4) and bake the pies for 30–35 minutes, or until golden brown on top. Remove the pies from the tins and leave to cool for a few minutes before serving.

ingredients

185 g (6½ oz) dried kidney beans

20 ml (½ fl oz/1 tablespoon) olive oil

6 garlic cloves, finely chopped

8 small red chillies, seeded and finely chopped

125 g (4½ oz) brown onions, chopped

1 kg (2 lb 4 oz) minced (ground) beef

65 g (2½ oz/⅔ cup) dry breadcrumbs

15 g (½ oz/3 teaspoons) white pepper

25 g (1 oz/1¼ tablespoons) salt

1 quantity puff pastry (see pages 162–5)

egg wash (see page 168), for brushing

chilli flakes, for sprinkling

beef and bean sausage rolls

makes 12

This sausage roll is a take on traditional chilli con carne. We developed it for our sister store, Central Baking Depot. The shop is in a part of Sydney's CBD that is being redeveloped and is filled with building sites. This beef and bean sausage roll is the builders' choice – rich beef mince with fresh chilli and lush red beans wrapped in flaky puff pastry — just what every strong man needs at nine in the morning.

method

Put the beans in a bowl, cover with water and set aside to soak overnight until softened. The following morning drain the beans and add 3 cups fresh water, bring to the boil and simmer until tender. Remove from the heat and allow to cool in the water. Drain well.

Heat the oil in a saucepan over medium heat. Add the garlic and chilli and cook for 2 minutes, or until aromatic. Add the onion and cook for 2–3 minutes, or until soft. Add the kidney beans and cook for a further 5 minutes, stirring until the flavours are combined. Remove from the heat and allow to cool.

Put the bean mixture in a large mixing bowl and add the beef, breadcrumbs, salt and white pepper. Using your hands, mix the meat quite forcefully for 3 minutes, to thoroughly combine (this will also work the protein in the meat).

Roll out the puff pastry into a rectangle, about 92 x 32 cm (36 x 12¾ inches). Cut the pastry into six rectangles about 15 x 30 cm (6 x 12 inches) each. Preheat the oven to 200°C (400°F/Gas 6).

Divide the filling mixture into six even-sized portions. On a clean work surface, roll each portion out into a 30 cm (12 inch) log with a 3 cm (1¼ inch) diameter. Place each log lengthways in the centre of a pastry rectangle and brush one long edge with egg wash. Firmly fold the pastry over, pressing to enclose the log tightly, leaving the ends open. Cut each roll into two even-sized halves and place on baking trays lined with baking paper, seam side down. Brush the top of each roll with egg wash and sprinkle with chilli flakes. Reduce the oven temperature to 190°C (375°F/Gas 5) and bake for 35–40 minutes, or until you cannot resist the smell any more and have to rip open the oven door and burn your mouth eating beans, meat and buttery pastry.

ingredients

100 g ($3\frac{1}{2}$ oz) sweet potato, peeled and cut into 1.5 cm ($\frac{5}{8}$ inch) cubes

40 ml ($1\frac{1}{4}$ fl oz/2 tablespoons) extra virgin olive oil

60 g ($2\frac{1}{4}$ oz) brown onions, finely chopped

5 garlic cloves, finely chopped

500 g (1 lb 2 oz) skinless boneless chicken thigh fillets, cut into 3 cm ($1\frac{1}{4}$ inch) pieces

200 g (7 oz) tomatoes, chopped

60 ml (2 fl oz/$\frac{1}{4}$ cup) verjuice

5 g ($\frac{1}{8}$ oz/1 teaspoon) salt

5 g ($\frac{1}{8}$ oz/1 teaspoon) freshly ground black pepper

4 g ($\frac{1}{8}$ oz/1 teaspoon) potato flour

50 g ($1\frac{3}{4}$ oz) lime pickle, finely chopped (see note)

80 g ($2\frac{3}{4}$ oz/$\frac{1}{2}$ cup) peas

1 large handful coriander leaves

1 quantity savoury shortcrust pastry (see pages 150–1)

$\frac{1}{2}$ quantity puff pastry (see page 162–5)

egg wash, for brushing (see page 168)

sesame seeds, for sprinkling

sweet potato, chicken and lime pickle pie

makes 6

It is tradition at Bourke Street Bakery that whenever we close the shop for renovations we indulge in lunch from Cleveland Street — a busy street in Surry Hills that is alive with Indian restaurants and only a two-minute walk from the bakery. This is how we fell in love with lime pickle, a beautiful affair to have, simultaneously sweet, salty and hot. Lime pickle is the predominant flavour in this chicken pie. It is made from limes that have been cut up and pickled with a variety of spices, such as garlic, ginger, turmeric and chilli.

method

Preheat the oven to 200°C (400°F/Gas 6). Put the sweet potato in a baking tray, drizzle with half of the oil, and cook in the oven for about 15 minutes, or until just before tender. Remove from the oven and set aside to cool.

Heat the remaining oil in a saucepan over medium heat. Add the onion and garlic and cook for 5 minutes, or until softened. Add the chicken pieces and cook for 5 minutes, or until the chicken has lost its pink colour. Add the tomato, verjuice, salt and pepper.

Pour enough water into the pan to cover the chicken. Bring to the boil, then reduce the heat and simmer for about 1 hour, or until the chicken is tender. Strain off the liquid into another saucepan, reserving the chicken mixture in a large container. Continue to cook the liquid over high heat until the liquid has reduced by one-third. Remove from the heat. Mix together the potato flour and 2 teaspoons water and add to the cooking liquid, stirring well to combine. Add the lime pickle and mix well to combine.

Add the roasted sweet potato, peas and coriander to the chicken mixture and stir well. Pour the cooking liquid back into the chicken mixture and mix thoroughly to combine. Allow to cool.

Roll out the savoury shortcrust pastry following the instructions on pages 150–1 and use it to line the base and sides of six 12.5 cm (4¾ inch) pie tins. Roll out the puff pastry following the instructions on pages 162–5 and cut out six circles with a 13.5 cm (5¼ inch) diameter to make the pie lids.

Spoon the mixture into the pastry-lined pie tins, filling them to the brim. To attach the puff pastry lids, brush the rim of the pastry base and lid with a little egg wash and lay the lid over the base. Pinch gently between your thumb and index finger to make a good seal around the circumference edge. Brush the top of the pie lid with egg wash, sprinkle with sesame seeds, and make a small hole in the middle to allow steam to escape. Reduce the oven temperature to 180°C (350°F/Gas 4) and bake the pies for 30–35 minutes, or until golden brown on top. Remove the pies from the tins and leave to cool a little before serving.

note

Lime pickle is mainly used in Indian cooking and can be purchased in jars from Indian grocery stores or a good supermarket. Use a medium lime pickle so the chilli will not be too overpowering.

ingredients

250 g (9 oz) dried chickpeas

40 ml (1¼ fl oz/2 tablespoons) olive oil

4 garlic cloves, finely chopped

100 g (3½ oz) brown onions, finely chopped

250 g (9 oz) red capsicums (peppers), seeded,
membrane removed and roughly chopped

1 small red chilli, seeded and finely chopped

1 teaspoon cumin seeds

1 teaspoon coriander seeds

800 g (1 lb 12 oz) baby English spinach

40 g (1½ oz/2 tablespoons) tahini

20 g (¾ oz) dry breadcrumbs

20 ml (½ fl oz/1 tablespoon) freshly squeezed lemon juice

20 g (¾ oz/1 tablespoon) plain yoghurt

1 large handful mint leaves, chopped

1 large handful coriander leaves, chopped

5 g (⅛ oz/1 teaspoon) salt

½ teaspoon cayenne pepper

1 quantity puff pastry (see pages 162–5)

egg wash (see page 168), for brushing

paprika, for sprinkling

chickpea rolls

makes 12

Bourke Street Bakery's chickpea roll is a take on a falafel roll. Falafel rolls are deep-fried chickpea or broad (fava) bean balls that are then stuffed into pita bread with salad. They have been around for thousands of years and are basically the Middle Eastern version of fast food.

Our chickpea roll has been around for considerably less time, although it is an even faster food. The chickpea roll does have a slight chilli heat, so if that is not to your liking, just omit the chilli. You can use English spinach or silverbeet (Swiss chard) instead of the baby spinach if you prefer.

method

Put the chickpeas in a bowl, cover with water and set aside to soak overnight to soften.

Drain the chickpeas and place them in a saucepan with 1 litre of water, place over high heat, bring to the boil then reduce to a simmer and cook until softened. Drain the chickpeas and blend with a stick blender or transfer to a food processor and process until mashed but not completely smooth — the mixture should be slightly chunky.

Heat the oil in a saucepan over medium heat. Add the garlic, onion, capsicum and chilli and cook for 3–4 minutes, or until soft. Add the cumin and coriander seeds and cook for 10 minutes, stirring regularly, until aromatic. Add the spinach, stir for 1 minute, or until slightly wilted, then remove from the heat. Allow to cool.

Transfer the spinach mixture to a large container and add the chickpeas, tahini, breadcrumbs, lemon juice, yoghurt, mint and coriander. Add the salt and cayenne pepper and stir well until all the ingredients are combined.

Roll out the puff pastry into a rectangle, about 92 x 32 cm (36 x 12¾ inches). Cut the pastry into six rectangles about 15 x 30 cm (6 x 12 inches) each. Preheat the oven to 200°C (400°F/Gas 6).

Divide the filling mixture into six even-sized portions. On a clean work surface, roll each portion out into a 30 cm (12 inch) log with a 3 cm (1¼ inch) diameter. Place each log lengthways in the centre of a pastry rectangle and brush one long edge with egg wash. Firmly fold the pastry over, pressing to enclose the log tightly, leaving the ends open. Cut each roll into two even-sized pieces and place on baking trays lined with baking paper, seam side down. Brush the top of each roll with egg wash and sprinkle with paprika. Reduce the oven temperature to 190°C (375°F/Gas 5) and bake for 35–40 minutes, or until golden brown.

ingredients

20 ml ($\frac{1}{2}$ fl oz/1 tablespoon) extra virgin olive oil

4 garlic cloves, finely chopped

50 g ($1\frac{3}{4}$ oz) brown onions, finely chopped

75 g ($2\frac{3}{4}$ oz) celery, cut into 1.5 cm ($\frac{5}{8}$ inch) pieces

2 rosemary sprigs, leaves picked

8 thyme sprigs, leaves picked

600 g (1 lb 5 oz) pork shoulder, cut into 2–3 cm ($\frac{3}{4}$–$1\frac{1}{4}$ inch) cubes (ask your butcher to do this)

250 g (9 oz) tomatoes, chopped

5 g ($\frac{1}{8}$ oz/1 teaspoon) salt

$2\frac{1}{2}$ g ($\frac{1}{8}$ oz/$\frac{1}{2}$ teaspoon) white pepper

110 g ($3\frac{3}{4}$ oz) apples, peeled, cored and cut into 1.5 cm ($\frac{5}{8}$ inch) cubes

150 g ($5\frac{1}{2}$ oz) red cabbage, shredded into 3 cm ($1\frac{1}{4}$ inch) lengths

4 g ($\frac{1}{8}$ oz/1 teaspoon) potato flour

1 quantity savoury shortcrust pastry (see pages 150–1)

$\frac{1}{2}$ quantity puff pastry (see page 162–5)

egg wash (see page 168), for brushing

fennel seeds, for sprinkling

pork, apple and braised red cabbage pie

makes 6

This pie tastes much better in winter. Do not even attempt to bake it unless it's below 18°C (64°F) outside with at least a light drizzle of rain.

method

Heat the oil in a saucepan over medium heat. Add the garlic, onion, celery, rosemary and thyme and cook for 5 minutes, or until the onion has softened. Add the pork and cook for 5 minutes, stirring occasionally until it has lost its pink colour. Add the tomato and enough water to cover the pork; then add the salt and pepper. Bring to the boil, then reduce the heat and simmer for about 1.5 hours, skimming any scum that rises to the surface and stirring every 30 minutes, until the pork is tender. Allow to cool.

Add the apple and cabbage to the saucepan and continue cooking for a further 15 minutes. Strain off the liquid into another saucepan, reserving the pork mixture in a large container. Continue to cook the liquid over high heat until reduced by one-third. Remove from the heat. Mix together the potato flour and 2 teaspoons water and add to the cooking liquid, then add the liquid to the pork mixture stirring well to combine.

Preheat the oven to 200°C (400°F/Gas 6). Roll out the savoury pastry following the instructions on pages 150–1 and use it to line the base and sides of six 12.5 cm (4¾ inch) pie tins. Roll out the puff pastry following the instructions on pages 162–5 and cut out six circles with a 13.5 cm (5¼ inch) diameter to make the pie lids.

Spoon the mixture into the pastry-lined pie tins, filling them to the brim. To attach the puff pastry lids, brush the rim of the pastry base and lid with a little egg wash and lay the lid over the base. Pinch gently between your thumb and index finger to make a good seal around the circumference edge. Brush the top of the pie lid with egg wash, sprinkle with fennel seeds, and make a small hole in the middle to allow steam to escape. Reduce the oven temperature to 180°C (350°F/Gas 4) and bake the pies for 30–35 minutes, or until golden brown on top. Remove the pies from the tins and leave to cool for a few minutes before serving.

ingredients

harissa (makes 400 g/14 oz)

5 red capsicums (peppers), seeded, membrane removed
and finely chopped

350 g (12 oz) brown onions, finely chopped

6 garlic cloves, finely chopped

2 small red chillies, finely chopped

1½ teaspoons coriander seeds

15 g (½ oz/3 teaspoons) smoked paprika

100 ml (3½ fl oz) water

75 g (2¾ oz) blanched almonds

1.2 kg (2 lb 10 oz) minced (ground) lamb

75 g (2¹³⁄₄ oz) couscous

110 g (3¾ oz/¾ cup) currants

20 g (¾ oz/1 tablespoon) salt

2½ g (⅛ oz/½ teaspoon) freshly ground black pepper

1 quantity puff pastry (see pages 162–5)

egg wash (see recipe, page 168), for brushing

poppy seeds, for sprinkling

lamb, harissa and almond sausage rolls makes 12

This sausage roll is a great mix of texture and flavour. When you bite into one of these rolls you should first smell the lamb, then taste the sweetness of the red capsicum with a little heat from the chilli, feel the crunch of the almonds and the squishy sweetness of the currants. All in all, quite yummy really.

Harissa is a north African chilli paste made traditionally from peppers, garlic, coriander and tomatoes. Ours is not strictly traditional but not far from it. This sausage roll also seems to have a deep affinity with pregnant women around Sydney. It is best to make the harissa first, which is very easy but requires some regular pot stirring.

method

To make the harissa, put the capsicum, onion, garlic, chilli, coriander seeds and paprika in a large saucepan over medium heat. Add the water and simmer for 2 hours, stirring every 10–20 minutes, or until reduced to a thick paste. As the mixture begins to reduce, the sugar will come out of the capsicum and will start sticking to the bottom of the pan, so you will need to keep a close eye on it and stir regularly. Remove from the heat and allow to cool. Weigh and set aside 350 g (12 oz/1½ cups) of the harissa to use in the sausage roll filling.

Preheat the oven to 200°C (400°F/Gas 6). Put the almonds on a baking tray and cook in the oven for 5 minutes, or until lightly golden. Roughly chop and add to a large mixing bowl with the lamb, couscous, currants, harissa, salt and pepper. Using your hands, mix the meat quite forcefully for 3 minutes, to thoroughly combine (this will also work the protein in the meat). The currants and couscous soak up the juices of the mix and will bind the filling together.

Roll out the puff pastry into a rectangle, about 92 x 32 cm (36 x 12¾ inches). Cut the pastry into six rectangles about 15 x 30 cm (6 x 12 inches) each.

Divide the filling mixture into six even-sized portions On a clean work surface, roll each portion out into a 30 cm (12 inch) log with a 3 cm (1¼ inch) diameter. Place each log lengthways in the centre of a pastry rectangle and brush one long edge with egg wash. Firmly fold the pastry over, pressing to enclose the log tightly, leaving the ends open. Cut each roll into two even-sized pieces and place on baking trays lined with baking paper, seam side down. Brush the top of each roll with egg wash and sprinkle with poppy seeds. Reduce the oven temperature to 190°C (375°F/Gas 5) and bake for 35–40 minutes, or until golden brown.

ingredients

40 ml (1¼ fl oz/2 tablespoons) extra virgin olive oil

200 g (7 oz) brown onions, finely chopped

5 garlic cloves, finely chopped

6 thyme sprigs

100 g (3½ oz) peeled and grated potato

55 ml (1¾ fl oz) verjuice

125 ml (4 fl oz/½ cup) water

800 g (1 lb 12 oz) baby English spinach

400 g (14 oz/1⅔ cups) ricotta cheese

200 g (7 oz/2 cups) grated parmesan cheese

1 handful basil leaves

8 g (¼ oz/1½ teaspoons) salt

5 g (⅛ oz/1 teaspoon) white pepper

1 quantity savoury shortcrust pastry (see page 150–1)

½ quantity puff pastry (see page 162–5)

egg wash (see page 168), for brushing

poppy seeds, for sprinkling

spinach and ricotta pie
makes 6

This is a classic vegetarian pie — everyone has a different version. At Bourke Street Bakery we have kept it fresh and simple, although for something different you can try adding a little ground nutmeg or cinnamon at the end. We use baby spinach in this recipe, but it works just as well with silverbeet (Swiss chard).

method

Heat the oil in a saucepan over medium heat. Add the onion and garlic and cook for 10 minutes, or until lightly browned. Add the thyme and cook for 2 minutes, stirring well. Add the potato, verjuice and water, cover with a lid and reduce the heat to low. Cook the potato for 10 minutes, stirring frequently, until it is partially cooked. Transfer to a large container and allow to cool.

Rinse the saucepan and return to medium heat. Add half of the spinach to the pan and cook for 1 minute, stirring often, until it has wilted. Remove from the pan and drain off any excess liquid in a colander. Repeat with the remaining spinach until it is all cooked. Cool slightly and squeeze the spinach to remove any excess liquid.

Add the spinach to the potato mixture with the ricotta cheese, parmesan cheese, basil, salt and pepper, stirring well to combine.

Preheat the oven to 200°C (400°F/Gas 6). Roll out the savoury pastry following the instructions on pages 150–1 and use it to line the base and sides of six 12.5 cm (4¾ inch) pie tins. Roll out the puff pastry following the instructions on pages 162–5 and cut out six circles with a 13.5 cm (5¼ inch) diameter to make the pie lids.

Spoon the mixture into the pastry-lined pie tins, filling them to the brim. To attach the puff pastry lids, brush the rim of the pastry base and lid with a little egg wash and lay the lid over the base. Pinch gently between your thumb and index finger to make a good seal around the circumference edge. Brush the top of the pie lid with egg wash, sprinkle with poppy seeds, and make a small hole in the middle to allow steam to escape. Reduce the oven temperature to 180°C (350°F/Gas 4) and bake the pies for 30–35 minutes, or until golden brown on top. Remove the pies from the tins and leave to cool for a few minutes before serving.

ingredients

30 ml (1 fl oz/1½ tablespoons) extra virgin olive oil

6 garlic cloves, finely chopped

40 g (1½ oz/3½ tablespoons) fennel seeds, finely chopped

4 thyme sprigs, leaves picked

150 g (5½ oz) brown onions, finely chopped

150 g (5½ oz) celery, finely chopped

150 g (5½ oz) carrots, finely chopped

1.2 kg (2 lb 10 oz) lean minced (ground) pork

40 g (1½ oz) dry breadcrumbs

20 g (¾ oz/1 tablespoon) salt

15 g (½ oz/3 teaspoons) white pepper

1 quantity puff pastry (see pages 162–5)

egg wash (see recipe, page 168), for brushing

fennel seeds, for sprinkling

pork and fennel sausage rolls
makes 12

Sydney's best butcher shops are filled with a multitude of gourmet sausages for sale and we have often thought that these flavours would taste far better wrapped in butter and flour than bung. (Bung, if you're wondering, is the name for sausage skin, which is made from animal intestine.)

Sydney's backyards are always alive with pork and fennel sausages rolling on barbecues, so we knew this sausage roll would be popular, but we never dreamed it would be this popular. Sydneysiders are addicted to them. In Surry Hills we are often asked if narcotics feature as an ingredient. But, as you can see above, we only use the best produce we can find (and besides, the food costs would just not allow it).

method

Heat the oil in a saucepan over medium heat. Add the garlic and cook for 30 seconds. Add the fennel seeds and thyme and stir together for 1 minute, or until aromatic. Add the onion and celery and cook for 5 minutes, or until the onion has softened. Add the carrots and cook for about 20 minutes, stirring often, until the vegetables are mushy. Remove from the heat and allow to cool.

Put the pork mince into a large bowl and add the cooled vegetables, breadcrumbs, salt and white pepper. Using your hands, mix the meat quite forcefully for 3 minutes to thoroughly combine (this will also work the protein in the meat). At this stage it is best to roll up a little ball of the meat mixture and cook it in a hot frying pan for 2 minutes to check the flavour. You may find it is too salty, however once the mix is encased in pastry the saltiness should even out. But if you cannot taste the salt at all then you need to add a pinch or two more.

Roll out the puff pastry into a rectangle, about 92 x 32 cm (36 x 12¾ inches). Cut the pastry into six rectangles about 15 x 30 cm (6 x 12 inches) each. Preheat the oven to 200°C (400°F/Gas 6).

Divide the filling mixture into six even-sized portions. On a clean work surface, roll each portion out into a 30 cm (12 inch) log with a 3 cm (1¼ inch) diameter. Place each log lengthways in the centre of a pastry rectangle and brush one long edge with egg wash. Firmly fold the pastry over, pressing to enclose the log tightly, leaving the ends open. Cut each roll into two even-sized pieces and place on baking trays lined with baking paper, seam side down. Brush the top of each roll with egg wash and sprinkle with fennel seeds. Reduce the oven temperature to 190°C (375°F/Gas 5) and bake for 35–40 minutes, or until they are a golden brown roll of steaming oozing goodness.

ingredients

500 g (1 lb 2 oz) eggplants (aubergines), cut into 2–3 cm ($^3/_4$–$1^1/_4$ inch) cubes

60 ml (2 fl oz/$^1/_4$ cup) extra virgin olive oil

8 garlic cloves, finely chopped

100 g ($3^1/_2$ oz) onion, finely chopped

600 g (1 lb 5 oz) red capsicums (peppers), seeded, membrane removed and chopped

300 g ($10^1/_2$ oz) tomatoes, chopped

100 ml ($3^1/_2$ fl oz) water

200 g (7 oz) green beans, trimmed and sliced into thirds

300 g ($10^1/_2$ oz) zucchini (courgettes), trimmed and cut into 1.5 cm ($^5/_8$ inch) pieces

100 g ($3^1/_2$ oz) preserved artichoke hearts, quartered

50 g ($1^3/_4$ oz/$^1/_2$ cup) grated parmesan cheese

5 g ($^1/_8$ oz/1 teaspoon) salt

5 g ($^1/_8$ oz/1 teaspoon) freshly ground black pepper

1 handful parsley leaves

1 handful basil leaves

1 quantity savoury shortcrust pastry (see pages 150–1)

$^1/_2$ quantity puff pastry (see page 162–5)

egg wash (see page 168), for brushing

nigella seeds, for sprinkling

ratatouille pie

makes 6

The vegetarian pie mixes at Bourke Street Bakery are made purely from vegetables. We wanted to keep our vegetarian pies clean and healthy so we decided not to bind the fillings with starch, flour or butter. The ratatouille pie was the first vegetarian pie we made and it still seems to invoke memories for the vegetarians of Surry Hills — one lady still stops us in the street to demand its return.

method

Preheat the oven to 220°C (425°F/Gas 7). Put the eggplant in a single layer on a tray and sprinkle with a little salt. Set aside for 10 minutes, then rinse well. Put the eggplant on a baking tray lined with baking paper, drizzle with half of the olive oil and cook for about 15–20 minutes, or until tender. Remove from the oven and set aside.

Heat the remaining oil in a frying pan over medium heat. Add the garlic and cook for 2 minutes, or until golden. Add the onion, capsicum and tomato. Pour in the water and season with salt and pepper. Bring to the boil, then reduce the heat and simmer for 45 minutes to 1 hour, stirring every 10 minutes or so — this mixture forms the binding agent for the pie so it needs to be quite thick. When it coats the back of a spoon use a stick blender to process until smooth. (If you don't have a stick blender, transfer the mixture to a food processor and process until smooth then pour back into the warm pan.)

Add the beans to the pan and cook for 2–3 minutes, then add the zucchini and cook for 10–15 minutes, or until the vegetables are tender. Remove from the heat and add to a bowl with the eggplant, artichoke hearts, parmesan, salt and pepper, stirring well to combine. Allow to cool, then stir through the parsley and basil before filling the pastry cases.

Preheat the oven to 200°C (400°F/Gas 6). Roll out the savoury pastry following the instructions on pages 150–1 and use it to line the base and sides of six 12.5 cm (4¾ inch) pie tins. Roll out the puff pastry following the instructions on pages 162–5 and cut out six circles with a 13.5 cm (5¼ inch) diameter to make the pie lids.

Spoon the mixture into the pastry-lined pie tins, filling them to the brim. To attach the puff pastry lids, brush the rim of the pastry base and lid with a little egg wash and lay the lid over the base. Pinch gently between your thumb and index finger to make a good seal around the circumference edge. Brush the top of the pie lid with egg wash, sprinkle with nigella seeds, and make a small hole in the middle to allow steam to escape. Reduce the oven temperature to 180°C (350°F/Gas 4) and bake the pies for 30–35 minutes, or until golden brown on top. Remove the pies from the tins and leave to cool for a few minutes before serving.

ingredients

75 g (2¾ oz/⅓ cup) chickpeas
500 ml (17 fl oz/2 cups) water
300 g (10½ oz) eggplants (aubergines)
70 ml (2¼ fl oz) extra virgin olive oil
60 g (2¼ oz) brown onions, finely
chopped
6 garlic cloves, finely chopped
½ teaspoon cumin seeds
600 g (1 lb 5 oz) minced (ground) lamb
150 g (5½ oz) plain yoghurt

finely grated zest of 2 lemons
5 g (⅛ oz/1 teaspoon) salt
2½ g (⅛ oz/½ teaspoon) white
pepper
4 g (⅛ oz/1 teaspoon) potato flour
1 large handful coriander leaves
1 quantity savoury shortcrust pastry
(see pages 150–1)
½ quantity puff pastry
(see pages 162–5)
egg wash (see page 168), for brushing

Mince pies are always a bit sloppy and this minced lamb pie is no exception. The degree of eating difficulty may be high, but the flavour makes it well worthwhile! You can also use lamb shoulder to make a chunkier pie or omit the pastry and make a delicious casserole instead.

lamb, chickpea & eggplant pie

makes 6

method

Put the chickpeas in a bowl and cover with water. Leave them to soak overnight, then drain well.

Place the drained chickpeas in a saucepan over high heat and add the water. Bring to the boil, then reduce the heat to low and simmer until just tender. Remove from the heat and allow to cool in the water. Drain well.

Cut the eggplants in half and place on a baking tray lined with baking paper, cut side down. Drizzle over half of the olive oil and cook in the oven for 20–30 minutes, or until softened. Allow to cool a little, then use a spoon to scoop out the flesh and discard the skin. Set aside.

Heat the remaining oil in a saucepan over medium heat. Add the onion and garlic and cook for 5 minutes, or until softened. Add the cumin seeds and cook for 2–3 minutes, stirring well. Add the lamb and cook for 5 minutes, stirring to break up any large lumps of meat. Add the yoghurt, lemon zest, salt and pepper.

Pour enough water into the pan to cover the lamb. Bring to the boil, then reduce the heat and simmer for 2 hours, skimming the scum from the surface and stirring every 30 minutes, until the lamb is tender.

Add the cooked chickpeas and eggplant to the lamb mixture and cook for about 5 minutes, stirring to combine, until all the flavours are incorporated. Strain off the liquid into another saucepan, reserving the mince mixture in a large container. Continue to cook the liquid over high heat until reduced by one-third. Remove from the heat. Mix together the potato flour and 2 teaspoons water and add to the cooking liquid, then add this to the lamb mixture and stir well. Stir through the coriander and adjust the seasoning if necessary. Allow to cool.

Preheat the oven to 200°C (400°F/Gas 6). Roll out the savoury pastry following the instructions on pages 150–1 and use it to line the base and sides of six 12.5 cm (4¾ inch) pie tins. Roll out the puff pastry following the instructions on pages 162–5 and cut out six circles with a 13.5 cm (5¼ inch) diameter to make the pie lids.

Spoon the mixture into the pastry-lined pie tins, filling them to the brim. To attach the puff pastry lids, brush the rim of the pastry base and lid with a little egg wash and lay the lid over the base. Pinch gently between your thumb and index finger to make a good seal around the circumference edge. Brush the top of the pie lid with egg wash and make a small hole in the middle to allow steam to escape. Reduce the oven temperature to 180°C (350°F/Gas 4) and bake the pies for 30–35 minutes, or until golden brown on top. Remove the pies from the tins and leave to cool for a few minutes before serving.

note

If you use lamb shoulder you will need to braise it for a little longer. If you do go down the casserole path, leave out the potato flour and reduce the seasoning a little.

ingredients

20 ml (½ fl oz/1 tablespoon) olive oil

2 garlic cloves, finely chopped

120 g (4¼ oz) brown onions, finely chopped

375 g (13 oz) bacon slices, finely chopped

250 g (9 oz) spring onions (scallions), chopped

1.2 kg (2 lb 10 oz) minced (ground) chicken

55 g (2 oz) dry breadcrumbs

10 g (¼ oz/2 teaspoons) salt

5 g (⅛ oz/1 teaspoon) white pepper

1 quantity puff pastry (see pages 162–5)

egg wash (see page 168), for brushing

sesame seeds, for sprinkling

This sausage roll is the ugly duckling of the three sausage roll sisters (the other two are the pork and fennel, and lamb) but for the staff it is the sausage roll of choice. It has a light and healthy feel, although it is unlikely to get a tick from the Heart Foundation anytime soon.

chicken and bacon sausage rolls
makes 12

method

Heat the oil in a saucepan over medium heat. Add the garlic and cook for 2 minutes. Add the onion and cook for 2–3 minutes, or until softened. Add the bacon and cook for 10 minutes, stirring regularly, or until aromatic. Remove from the heat and stir through the spring onions. Allow to cool.

Put the bacon mixture in a large mixing bowl and add the chicken, breadcrumbs, salt and white pepper. Using your hands, mix the meat quite forcefully for 3 minutes — this will also work the protein in the meat.

Roll out the puff pastry into a rectangle, about 92 x 32 cm (36 x 12¾ inches). Cut the pastry into six rectangles about 15 x 30 cm (6 x 12 inches) each. Preheat the oven to 200°C (400°F/Gas 6).

Divide the filling mixture into six even-sized portions. On a clean work surface, roll each portion out into a 30 cm (12 inch) log with a 3 cm (1¼ inch) diameter. Place each log lengthways in the centre of a pastry rectangle and brush one long edge with egg wash. Firmly fold the pastry over, pressing to enclose the log tightly, leaving the ends open. Cut each roll into two pieces and place on the tray, seam side down. Brush the tops with egg wash and sprinkle with sesame seeds. Reduce the oven temperature to 190°C (375°F/Gas 5) and bake for 35–40 minutes, or until golden brown and oozing chicken juice.

ingredients

pickled quinces

500 g (1 lb 2 oz) caster (superfine) sugar

1 litre (35 fl oz/4 cups) white wine vinegar

6 juniper berries

4 cloves

5 whole peppercorns

6 quinces, peeled, cored and quartered

1.5 kg (3 lb 5 oz) rabbit, cleaned and cut into 3 cm (1¼ inch) pieces, reserving the bones (ask your butcher to do this)

1 bay leaf

1 celery, chopped

1 carrot, chopped

30 ml (1 fl oz/1½ tablespoons) extra virgin olive oil

100 g (3½ oz) red onions, finely chopped

10 garlic cloves, finely chopped

6 juniper berries

20 thyme sprigs, leaves picked

100 g (3½ oz) celery, finely chopped

100 g (3½ oz) pearl barley

½ teaspoon potato flour

5 g (⅛ oz/1 teaspoon) salt

2½ g (⅛ oz/½ teaspoon) freshly ground black pepper

1 quantity savoury shortcrust pastry (see pages 150–1)

½ quantity puff pastry (see pages 162–5)

egg wash (see page 168), for brushing

cumin seeds, for sprinkling

rabbit and quince pie

makes 6

Most of the products at the Bakery we tailor to customers' tastes, as at the end of the day we want everyone to enjoy our food. Every now and then we make something that we know is not going to be a bestseller, but we make it anyway because we want to try different things to challenge ourselves, always with the hope that we will stumble onto something unique and truly tasty. This pie is one of those efforts.

This rabbit pie was made especially for the Easter holiday. Bugs Bunny would have been happy to die for this pie and in his pastry grave he would have no greater friend than in-season quinces.

method

To make the pickled quince, put the sugar, white wine vinegar, juniper berries, cloves and peppercorns into a heavy stainless steel saucepan over medium heat. Add the quince quarters, bring to the boil, then reduce the heat and simmer for 2 hours, or until tender but firm. Remove the quince quarters from the pan and set aside to cool. The cooking syrup can be poured over any left-over quince and stored in a sterilised airtight jar. It will keep in the refrigerator for up to 3 months and can be used to accompany cheese or as a garnish for pâté or salad.

Put the rabbit bones in a large saucepan with the bay leaf, celery and carrot. Cover with 2.5 litres (87 fl oz/10 cups) water and bring to the boil, then reduce the heat and simmer for 1 hour, or until aromatic. Strain the stock, discarding the bones, and set aside.

Heat the oil in a frying pan over medium heat. Add the onion and garlic and cook for 5 minutes, or until softened. Add the juniper berries, thyme, celery and rabbit meat and cook for 5 minutes, or until the rabbit has lost its pink colour. Pour in enough stock to cover the rabbit and bring to the boil, then reduce the heat and simmer for $1^1/_2$ hours until the meat is nearly tender.

Add the barley to the pan and continue cooking over low heat for about 30 minutes, or until the meat and barley are tender. Strain off the liquid into another saucepan, reserving the rabbit mixture in a large container. Measure the cooking liquid — an ideal amount is 200 ml (7 fl oz). If you have more than this continue to cook the liquid over high heat until reduced. Mix together the potato flour and 2 teaspoons water and add to the cooking liquid. Pour the sauce over the rabbit mixture, add the salt and pepper, and stir through with the quince. Allow to cool.

Preheat the oven to 200°C (400°F/Gas 6). Roll out the savoury pastry following the instructions on pages 150–1 and use it to line the base and sides of six 12.5 cm ($4^3/_4$ inch) pie tins. Roll out the puff pastry following the instructions on pages 162–5 and cut out six circles with a 13.5 cm ($5^1/_4$ inch) diameter to make the pie lids.

Spoon the mixture into the pastry-lined pie tins, filling them to the brim. To attach the puff pastry lids, brush the rim of the pastry base and lid with a little egg wash and lay the lid over the base. Pinch gently between your thumb and index finger to make a good seal around the circumference edge. Brush the top of the pie lid with egg wash, sprinkle with cumin seeds, and make a small hole in the middle to allow steam to escape. Reduce the oven temperature to 180°C (350°F/Gas 4) and bake the pies for 30–35 minutes, or until golden brown on top. Remove the pies from the tins and leave to cool for a few minutes before serving.

ingredients

2 quantities sweet shortcrust pastry
(see pages 152–7)

6 pears, peeled, cored and cut into
1 cm (½ inch) cubes

40 g (1½ oz) unsalted butter cut into
1 cm (½ inch) cubes

50 g (1¾ oz) soft brown sugar

¼ teaspoon ground cinnamon

2 teaspoons freshly squeezed
lemon juice

185 g (6½ oz) blueberries

egg wash (see page 168)

It is a treat eating one of these pies straight from the oven. These little pies are baked in a pastry shell that has not been blind baked first. The pears are roasted in brown sugar and a little cinnamon to intensify the flavour and evaporate some of the juices that ooze from the fruit as it cooks.

pear and blueberry pies makes 20

method

Roll out the pastry following the instructions on pages 152–7 and line twenty 8 cm (3¼ inch) round fluted loose-based tart tins. Cut out twenty circles with a 9 cm (3½ inch) diameter to use for the lids. Set the pastry cases and lids in the freezer for at least 20 minutes. Preheat the oven to 200°C (400°F/Gas 6).

Put the pears in a bowl and add the butter, sugar, cinnamon and lemon juice, tossing well to combine. Place them into a baking dish that holds them snugly in a layer no more than 2 cm (¾ inch) deep. Cook in the oven for 12 minutes, or until softened but still holding their shape. Remove from the oven, transfer to a bowl and add the blueberries while the pears are still warm, mixing well. Allow to cool to room temperature, then drain in a colander.

Spoon 2½ tablespoons of the fruit mixture into each tart shell, piling it slightly higher than the top of the shell.

To attach the lids, brush the rim of the pastry base and the lid with a little egg wash and lay the lid over the base. Squeeze gently between your thumb and index finger to make a good seal. Brush the tops with egg wash and make a small hole in the middle to allow steam to escape. Sprinkle a little caster sugar on top and place the pies on baking trays. Reduce the oven temperature to 180°C (350°F/Gas 4) and cook the pies for 20–25 minutes, or until the pastry is a deep golden colour. These pies are best served hot but can also be eaten cold.

ingredients

75 g (2¾ oz/½ cup) currants

75 g (2¾ oz) raisins

30 g (1 oz) mixed peel (mixed candied citrus peel)

2 tablespoons brandy

80 ml (2½ fl oz/⅓ cup) apple cider

50 g (1¾ oz) unsalted butter

75 g (2¾ oz) soft brown sugar

¼ teaspoon mixed (pumpkin pie) spice

¼ teaspoon ground cinnamon

300 g (10½ oz) apples, cored, peeled and cut into 5 mm (¼ inch) cubes

25 g (1 oz) blanched almonds, roughly chopped

finely grated zest of ½ lemon

juice of ½ lemon

1 quantity sweet pastry (pâté sablée), (see page 159)

caster (superfine) sugar, for sprinkling

christmas fruit mince pies
makes 20

Dried fruit soaked in alcohol plays a big part in most sweet Christmas recipes and these fruit mince pies are no exception. At Bourke Street Bakery we use the very buttery pâté sablée, which melts in your mouth. These aren't the type of fruit mince tarts that can sit in your cupboard or refrigerator for weeks leading up to Christmas, although they will keep for up to 5 days in the refrigerator and can be frozen for up to 3 weeks. For best results, bake and eat as soon as the tarts are cool. You will need to soak the fruit for 1 week before making.

method

Put the currants, raisins and mixed peel in a bowl and pour over the brandy and apple cider, mixing well to coat. Cover with plastic wrap and set aside for at least 1 week.

Melt the butter in a frying pan over medium heat and add the brown sugar, mixed spice and cinnamon, stirring well. Add the apple and cook for 2–3 minutes, or until softened but holding their shape. Remove from the heat and fold into the macerated fruit. Add the almonds, lemon zest and juice, mixing well to combine.

Brush twenty 6.5 cm ($2^2/_3$ inch) individual tart tins with a little butter. Roll out the pastry following the instructions on page 159 and cut out the bases to line the tins. Re-roll the pastry as needed to cut out twenty lids.

Preheat the oven to 170°C (325°F/Gas 3). Place about $2^1/_2$ teaspoons of fruit mince into the base of each tart. To attach the lids, brush the rim of the pastry base and the lid with a little egg wash and lay the lid over the base. Squeeze gently between your thumb and index finger to make a good seal. Make a small hole in the middle to allow steam to escape and sprinkle a little caster sugar over the top of each pie. Bake the pies for 20 minutes, or until the tops are golden.

note

You can re-bake cooked frozen tarts in a 150°C (300°F/Gas 2) oven for 12 minutes before serving.

ingredients

1 quantity empanada dough
(see page 161)

120 g (4¼ oz) dried chickpeas

400 g (14 oz) eggplants (aubergines),
cut into 5 mm (¼ inch) cubes

50 ml (1¾ fl oz/2½ tablespoons) olive oil

2 garlic cloves, finely chopped

100 g (3½ oz) brown onions, finely
chopped

150 g (5½ oz) goat's curd

300 g (10½ oz) tomatoes, cut into
5 mm (¼ inch) cubes

1 small handful coriander leaves,
finely grated zest of ½ lemon

2 hard-boiled eggs, finely chopped

2 teaspoons paprika

5 g (⅛ oz/1 teaspoon) salt

egg wash (see page 168),
for brushing

chickpea, goat's curd and eggplant empanadas makes 12

method

Put the chickpeas in a bowl and cover with water. Set aside to soak overnight.

Roll out the empanada dough following the instructions on page 161 and cut twelve circles with a 14 cm (5½ inch) diameter.

Drain the chickpeas and put them in a saucepan over high heat. Cover with water and bring to the boil. Reduce the heat to medium and simmer until tender. Drain. Use the back of a knife or a mortar and pestle to mash half of the chickpeas, then mix them back in with the whole chickpeas.

Put the eggplant on a tray and sprinkle with some extra salt. Set aside for about 10 minutes, then rinse well.

Heat the oil in a frying pan over mƒedium heat and add the eggplant. Cook for 5 minutes, or until tender and crisp. Add the garlic and cook for 4 minutes, or until golden. Add the onion and cook for 5 minutes, or until softened. Remove from the heat and set aside to cool. Add the eggplant to the chickpeas with the goat's curd, tomato, coriander, lemon zest, egg, paprika and salt and stir well to combine.

Preheat the oven to 250°C (500°F/Gas 9). Put 2–3 tablespoons of the filling into the centre of each pastry circle. Fold the pastry over and use a fork to press down around the edges to seal. Brush with the egg wash and place on a baking tray lined with baking paper.

Reduce the heat to 230°C (450°F/Gas 8) and cook the empanadas in the oven for 20 minutes, turning the tray around after 10 minutes, or until golden. Serve hot.

ingredients

1 quantity empanada dough (see page 161)

110 g (3¾ oz) suet (see note, page 161)

6 garlic cloves , finely chopped

120 g (4¼ oz) brown onions, finely chopped

650 g (1 lb 7 oz) minced (ground) beef

1 long red chilli, seeded and finely chopped

90 g (3¼ oz/¾ cup) raisins

110 g (3¾ oz/½ cup) green olives, pitted and finely chopped

1 teaspoon paprika

7 g (¼ oz/1½ teaspoons) salt

1 small handful parsley leaves

2 hard-boiled eggs, finely chopped

egg wash (see page 168), for brushing

beef empanadas makes 12

method

Roll out the empanada dough following the instructions on page 161 and cut twelve circles with a 14 cm (5½ inch) diameter.

Melt the suet in a frying pan over low heat then strain and return the rendered suet to the pan — you should have about 75 ml (2¼ fl oz) once rendered. Increase the heat to medium and add the garlic. Cook for 1 minute, or until golden. Add the onion and cook for 3–4 minutes, or until softened, then add the beef and cook for 5 minutes, breaking up any larger pieces of meat with a wooden spoon. Add the chilli, raisins, olives, paprika and salt and cook for a further 5 minutes, stirring to combine. Remove from the heat, place the mixture in a bowl and mix through the parsley and egg. Set aside to cool.

Preheat the oven to 250°C (500°F/Gas 9). Put 2–3 tablespoons of the filling into the centre of each pastry circle. Fold the pastry over and use a fork to press down on the edges to seal. Brush with the egg wash and place on a baking tray lined with baking paper.

Reduce the heat to 230°C (450°F/Gas 8) and cook the empanadas in the oven for 20 minutes, turning the tray around after 10 minutes, or until golden. Serve hot.

tarts

A crisp shell with a luscious filling epitomises a great tart. To achieve this. the tarts at Bourke Street Bakery are made numerous times throughout the day. Customers have come to expect pastries that are no more than a few hours old. Some customers have admitted to serving up our tarts to guests claiming them to be their own creations. With the following recipes we now offer this opportunity to all without the guilt.

ingredients

1 quantity savoury shortcrust pastry
(see page 150–1)

35 g (1¼ oz) butter

1 large leek (about 200 g/7 oz), white
part only, washed and finely sliced

80 ml (2½ fl oz/⅓ cup) white wine

300 ml (10½ fl oz) pouring (whipping)
cream (35% fat)

300 g (10½ oz) soft goat's cheese

4 eggs

3 thyme sprigs, leaves picked

½ teaspoon salt

½ teaspoon freshly ground black pepper

Sunday brunch, sitting under the grapevines on the terrace watching the river flow in the distance, glass of Semillon in hand, a pear and rocket salad with croutons and a goat's cheese and leek tart. Drop a couple of roast tomatoes or field mushrooms sautéed in butter and parsley on top of the tarts before popping them in the oven if you so desire.

goat's cheese and leek tart

makes 8

method

Preheat the oven to 220°C (425°F/Gas 7). Roll out the savoury pastry following the instructions on pages 150–1 and use it to line the base and sides of eight 10 cm (4 inch) fluted, loose-based tart tins. Place in the refrigerator.

Melt the butter in a frying pan over medium heat and sauté the leek for about 5 minutes, or until softened. Add the wine, swish it around, and allow it to evaporate completely. Remove from the heat and set aside.

Heat the cream in a saucepan over medium heat and crumble the goat's cheese into it, stirring continuously until the cheese has completely dissolved and the cream thickens. Remove from the heat and set aside.

Put the eggs in the bowl of an electric mixer fitted with a whisk attachment and mix for about 3 minutes on high speed, or until light and fluffy. Add the cream mixture, thyme, salt and pepper, and continue mixing on low speed for about 30 seconds to combine.

Put the pastry shells on a baking tray lined with baking paper and scatter the cooled leeks into the shells. Pour over the cream mixture to fill each tart. Slide the tray onto the middle shelf of the oven, reduce the oven temperature to 180°C (350°F/Gas 4) and bake for 30–35 minutes, or until golden. Remove from the oven and allow to cool a little before serving.

1 quantity savoury shortcrust pastry
(see pages 150–1)

12 asparagus spears, trimmed and
cut into 5 cm (2 inch) pieces

8 eggs

400 ml (14 fl oz) pouring (whipping)
cream (35% fat)

2½ g (¹⁄₁₆ oz/½ teaspoon) salt

240 g (8¾ oz) gruyère
cheese, grated

4 tarragon sprigs, leaves picked and
roughly chopped

freshly ground black pepper,
to taste

Originally, the quiche was savoury egg custard baked in a
pastry shell with bacon. Today, any combination of vegetable,
or occasionally meat fillings, baked in a savoury custard is
called a quiche. Come up with your own combinations, but
remember to keep it simple and don't try to add too many
flavours — the custard is the star of the show. Take care not
to overcook the custard, it should be rich and silky. Just like
boiling an egg, if you cook it for a minute too long the result
will be very different to the one that could have been.

asparagus and gruyère quiches

makes 8

method

Roll out the savoury pastry following the instructions on pages 150–1 and use
it to line the base and sides of eight 10 cm (4 inch) fluted, loose-based tart
tins. Place in the refrigerator. Preheat the oven to 220°C (425°F/Gas 7).

Blanch the asparagus in a saucepan of boiling water for 1 minute, then
immediately plunge into a bowl of cold water. Drain and set aside.

Put the eggs, cream and salt in a bowl and whisk together using a fork.
Place the pastry shells on a baking tray. Scatter the asparagus and gruyère
cheese evenly between the pastry cases and then sprinkle over the tarragon
leaves. Pour over the egg custard to fill each tart as much as possible without
overflowing. Season with pepper, to taste. Slide the tray onto the middle shelf
of the oven, reduce the oven temperature to 170°C (325°F/Gas 3) and bake for
about 30–35 minutes, or until the custard is just set and starting to colour on
top. Remove from the oven and allow to cool a little before serving.

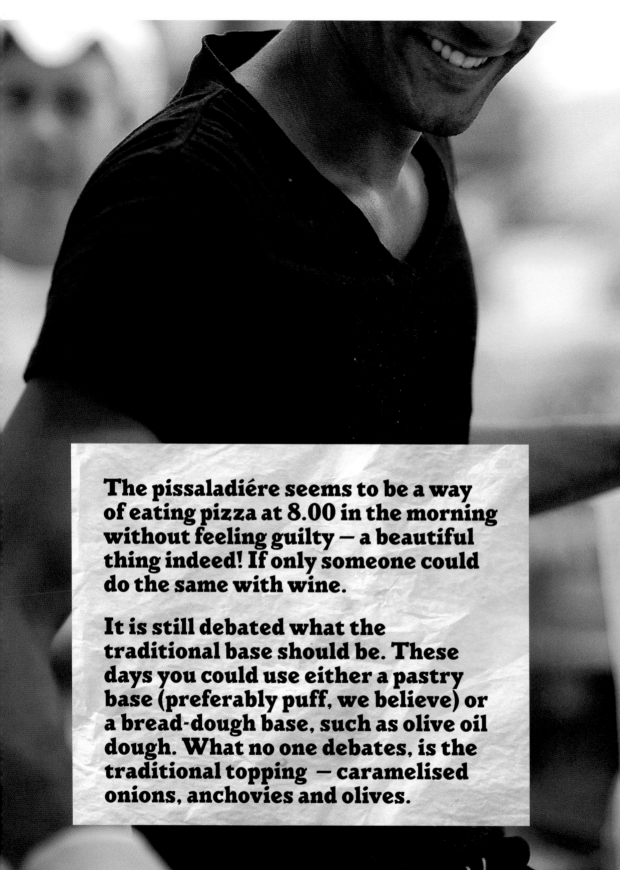

The pissaladiére seems to be a way of eating pizza at 8.00 in the morning without feeling guilty — a beautiful thing indeed! If only someone could do the same with wine.

It is still debated what the traditional base should be. These days you could use either a pastry base (preferably puff, we believe) or a bread-dough base, such as olive oil dough. What no one debates, is the traditional topping — caramelised onions, anchovies and olives.

1 quantity puff pastry (see pages 162–5)

egg wash (see page 168), for brushing

250 g (9 oz/1 cup) caramelised onion (see page 134)

6 prosciutto slices

6 fresh figs, quartered

90 g (3¼ oz) gorgonzola cheese

30 ml (1 fl oz/1½ tablespoons) olive oil

During the 14th century the French decided to break away with two equally important staples of Italian life — the papacy and the pizza. The Antipope was set up in Avignon where Roman cooks most probably taught the French a little something about pizza. The French adapted the pizza to taste, and what survives is the pissaladière.

fig, prosciutto and gorgonzola pissaladière makes 6

method

To make the bases, roll out the puff pastry to make a 25 x 38 cm (10 x 15 inch) rectangle, about 3 mm (⅛ inch) thick. Trim the edges and cut the pastry into 12 cm (4½ inch) squares — you should make six squares in total. Remember, when cutting puff pastry do not drag the knife through the pastry, cut the pastry from the top down. Lay the squares on a baking tray lined with baking paper, leaving a 3 cm (1¼ inch) space between each one. Brush the edges of each square with egg wash.

Preheat the oven to its highest temperature. Spread 2 tablespoons of caramelised onion over each square, leaving a 2 cm (¾ inch) border around the edges. Lay a single piece of prosciutto over the onion and arrange four fig quarters on top. Scatter over pieces of gorgonzola and drizzle with olive oil.

Cook the pissaladière for 15 minutes, turning the tray after 10 minutes, until the base is cooked through. Allow to cool slightly on the trays before serving.

variation

You can make canapés by cutting the pastry into 4 cm (1½ inch) squares and adjust the toppings. Cook for 10 minutes in a 180°C (350°F/Gas 4) oven.

ingredients

1 quantity puff pastry (see page 162–5)

egg wash (see page 168), for brushing

2 red capsicums (peppers)

250 g (9 oz/1 cup) caramelised onions (see page 134)

18 anchovies

24 pitted green olives, halved

120 g (4¼ oz) soft goat's cheese

30 ml (1 fl oz/1½ tablespoons) olive oil

red capsicum, anchovy, olive and goat's cheese pissaladière

makes 6

method

To make the bases, roll out the puff pastry to make a 25 x 38 cm (10 x 15 inch) rectangle, about 3 mm (⅛ inch) thick. Trim the edges and cut the pastry into 12 cm (4½ inch) squares — you should make six squares in total. Remember, when cutting puff pastry do not drag the knife through the pastry, cut the pastry from the top down. Lay the squares on a baking tray lined with baking paper, leaving a 3 cm (1¼ inch) space between each one. Brush the edges of each square with egg wash.

Cut the capsicums into quarters and remove the seeds and membrane. Place the capsicums, skin side up, under a hot grill (broiler) and grill until the skins blacken. Cool in a plastic bag, peel the skin and cut the flesh into strips.

Preheat the oven to its highest temperature. Spread 2 tablespoons of caramelised onion over each pastry square, leaving a 2 cm (¾ inch) border around the edges. Lay three anchovies across the centre, then lay four strips of red capsicum on top, making a criss-cross pattern. Scatter with the olives and pieces of the goat's cheese and drizzle with the olive oil.

Cook the pissaladière for 15 minutes, turning the tray after 10 minutes, until the base is cooked through. Allow to cool slightly on the trays before serving.

note

Use up any scraps of puff pastry by brushing them with a little olive oil and sprinkling with salt and pepper, even a little cheese, then cook them in a 180°C (350°F/Gas 4) oven for 10 minutes, or until golden.

ingredients

1 quantity puff pastry (see pages 162–5)

egg wash (see page 168), for brushing

600 g (1 lb 5 oz) in-season mushrooms

125 ml (4 fl oz/½ cup) olive oil

3 rosemary sprigs, leaves picked

8 thyme sprigs, leaves picked

250 g (9 oz/1 cup) caramelised onion (see page 134)

2 balls of buffalo mozzarella, cut into thirds

mushroom and herb pissaladière

makes 6

method

To make the bases, roll out the puff pastry to make a 25 x 38 cm (10 x 15 inch) rectangle, about 3 mm (⅛ inch) thick. Trim the edges and cut the pastry into 12 cm (4½ inch) squares — you should make six squares in total. Remember, when cutting puff pastry do not drag the knife through the pastry, cut the pastry from the top down. Lay the squares on a baking tray lined with baking paper, leaving a 3 cm (1¼ inch) space between each one. Brush the edges of each square with egg wash.

Preheat the oven to its highest temperature. To clean the mushrooms, remove the stalk and if they are covered in dirt run them under cold water. Use a small brush to paint the mushrooms with olive oil and place on a baking tray lined with baking paper. Sprinkle the rosemary and thyme over the mushrooms and cook in the oven for 7–10 minutes, or until the mushrooms are almost tender. Set aside and allow to cool.

Spread 2 tablespoons of caramelised onion over each pastry piece, leaving a 2 cm (¾ inch) border around the edges. Divide the mushrooms between the squares — if they are too big, cut them in half and arrange them over the onions. Season with salt and freshly ground black pepper, to taste.

Cook the pissaladière for 15 minutes, turning the tray after 10 minutes, until the base is cooked through. Allow to cool slightly on the trays before serving.

ingredients

10 eggs

200 g (7 oz) caster (superfine) sugar

250 ml (9 fl oz/1 cup) freshly squeezed lemon juice

300 ml (10½ fl oz) pouring (whipping) cream (35% fat)

1 quantity sweet shortcrust pastry (see pages 152–7)

This is a baked lemon tart filling that we cook in a double-boiler, resulting in a silky smooth curd. To make passionfruit curd instead, the lemon juice can be replaced with strained passionfruit juice.

lemon curd tarts
makes 20

method

To make the lemon curd filling, put the eggs, sugar and lemon juice in a stainless steel bowl. Use a whisk to mix together for 2–4 minutes, or until the sugar dissolves. Pour in the cream and mix well to combine. Place the bowl over a saucepan of simmering water and use a whisk to stir continuously for about 10 minutes, or until the mixture is smooth and thick. Have a rubber spatula on hand to scrape down the sides of the bowl as you work. The curd should transform as it cooks, starting off as a very thin cream with froth on top that will then become thick with bubbles. These bubbles will disappear altogether about 5 minutes before cooking is complete. Most importantly, keep stirring at all times or you may end up with a grainy texture in the finished curd. When the mixture is cooked, remove from the heat, stir for about 1 minute longer to cool a little, then place plastic wrap directly onto the top of the curd and refrigerate for at least 8 hours, or overnight.

Follow the instructions on pages 152–7 to roll out the pastry and use it to line twenty 8 cm (3¼ inch) round fluted loose-based tart tins. Set the pastry cases in the freezer for at least 20 minutes.

Blind bake the tart cases in a preheated 200°C (400°F/Gas 6) oven for 20–25 minutes, or until golden. Remove from the oven and allow to cool.

Using a piping (icing) bag fitted with a small plain nozzle, pipe about 2 tablespoons of the lemon curd into each tart shell and serve.

1 quantity sweet shortcrust pastry (see pages 152–7)

850 g (1 lb 14 oz) good-quality milk chocolate, finely chopped

500 ml (17 fl oz/2 cups) pouring (whipping) cream (35% fat)

The difference between these chocolate ganache tarts and most other chocolate ganache tarts is that we use milk chocolate instead of dark chocolate. Milk chocolate isn't as rich, making it possible for even a non-chocoholic to consume a full tart in a few quick mouthfuls.

chocolate ganache tarts

makes 20

method

Follow the instructions on pages 152–7 to roll out the pastry and use it to line twenty 8 cm (3¼ inch) round fluted loose-bottomed tart tins. Set the pastry cases in the freezer for at least 20 minutes.

Blind bake the tart cases in a preheated 200°C (400°F/Gas 6) oven for 20–25 minutes, or until golden. Remove from the oven and allow to cool.

To make the chocolate filling, put the chocolate into a stainless steel bowl. Put the cream in a saucepan and bring to the boil over high heat — this needs to happen quickly so the cream doesn't evaporate and reduce in volume. Pour the cream over the chocolate and stir with a rubber spatula or a wooden spoon until well combined. Be careful not to create air bubbles, as these will give a pocked look to the top of the tarts.

Pour the chocolate mixture into a jug and then pour into the baked tart shells until filled to the brim.

Allow the tarts to set at room temperature overnight in a plastic airtight container. These chocolate tarts are best not refrigerated and should be eaten within 24 hours. If you do need to keep them for longer, they can be refrigerated for up to 2 days, then brought back to room temperature to be eaten, but condensation will form on the top after refrigeration, which will affect their appearance.

ingredients

720 ml (25 fl oz) pouring (whipping) cream (35% fat)

5 cm (2 inch) piece ginger, finely sliced

1 cardamom pod, bruised

½ cinnamon stick

10 egg yolks

80 g (2¾ oz/⅓ cup) caster (superfine) sugar, plus extra for burning

1 quantity sweet shortcrust pastry (see page 152–7)

1½ tablespoons pistachios, chopped

ginger brûlée tarts
makes 20

The idea behind this tart came about many years ago when I was travelling through the Indian Himalayas. It was here that I first tasted the flavours of masala chai, the spiced sweet milky tea that is drunk in all chai shops in India. At first I wanted to make a custard flavoured with these spices and years later, when the Bakery opened its doors, I did, only by then it had morphed into a chai spiced brûlée. Although we call it the ginger brûlée tart, it actually contains some of the spices commonly used in masala chai and is a popular favourite at the Bakery.

This tart filling is one of the most challenging in the book — the brûlée filling is easy to overcook and easy to undercook. This version of the filling uses pouring cream with a 35 per cent fat content, which results in a softer filling than the one we produce at the Bakery, where we use a cream with 45 per cent fat that is often hard to find in shops.

method

Put the cream into a saucepan over high heat and add the ginger, cardamom and cinnamon stick. As soon as it boils, remove from the heat, pour into a large container or bowl, cover with plastic wrap, and place in the refrigerator overnight for the flavours to infuse.

Reheat the infused cream in a saucepan over medium–high heat, bring to simmering point, then remove from the heat. Set aside until needed.

Place the egg yolks in a stainless steel bowl and use a whisk to combine. Add the sugar and continue whisking for about 30 seconds, or until the sugar has dissolved. Pour the warmed cream through a fine sieve, discarding the spices, then pour the cream into the egg yolk mixture, whisking well to combine.

Put the bowl over a saucepan of simmering water, making sure the base of the bowl does not touch the water, and continue stirring with a whisk for about 10–15 minutes, or until the mixture is smooth and thick, scraping down the sides of the bowl regularly with a rubber spatula. It is important to keep stirring at all times or the mixture will curdle. Remove the bowl from the heat and whisk briskly for about 2 minutes to cool it quickly. Over the next 1 hour, whisk the mixture every 10 minutes until cooled. Use a rubber spatula to clean the side of the bowl thoroughly and place plastic wrap directly on top of the mixture; refrigerate overnight to set.

Follow the instructions on pages 152–7 to roll out the pastry and use it to line twenty 8 cm (3¼ inch) round fluted loose-based tart tins. Set the pastry cases in the freezer for at least 20 minutes.

Blind bake the tart cases in a preheated 200°C (400°F/Gas 6) oven for 20–25 minutes, or until golden. Remove from the oven and allow to cool.

Pipe the custard into the tart shells with a piping (icing) bag fitted with a plain nozzle — you should just slightly overfill the filling in each one. With a small pallet knife, scrape the custard to be flush with the top of the tart shell. Place in the refrigerator to set for 4 hours.

Sprinkle about 1 teaspoon caster sugar over the top of each tart and burn with a blowtorch to caramelise the top. Sprinkle a few pistachios on top to serve.

variation

If you prefer, you can omit the blowtorch step and serve the tarts simply with the ginger custard — just sprinkle a few pistachios directly onto the custard to serve.

ingredients

chocolate mousse (makes 3 cups)

200 g (7 oz/1⅓ cups) finely chopped dark chocolate (55% cocoa)

300 ml (10½ fl oz) pouring (whipping) cream (35% fat)

3 egg yolks

25 g (1 oz) caster (superfine) sugar for egg yolks

2 egg whites

10 g (¼ oz/2 teaspoons) caster (superfine) sugar for egg whites

raspberry purée

125 g (4½ oz/1 cup) raspberries

65 g (2½ oz) caster (superfine) sugar

1 quantity sweet shortcrust pastry (see pages 152–7)

½ cup chocolate cake crumbs (see page 307)

chocolate mousse tarts

makes 20

This scrumptious tart combines two of the most compatible dessert flavours — chocolate and raspberries. A dollop of raspberry purée hidden in the bottom of the tart offers a nice surprise for first-time indulgers. The cake crumbs on the top offer an extra chocolatey crunch. The chocolate mousse is perfect for many uses as a dessert and can be served in a martini glass with fresh berries and cream to make a great old-school finish to a meal. It could also be used as a cream layer in a chocolate cake.

To make the chocolate mousse component really work you have to get everything ready at the one time. It takes some practice, but as with all chocolate recipes, if you use a good-quality chocolate and don't burn it, the result will be more than acceptable. If you are short on time, then you can omit the cake crumbs and serve with fresh raspberries instead.

method

To make the chocolate mousse, put the chocolate and 100 ml (3½ fl oz) of the cream in a stainless steel bowl. Bring a saucepan of water to the boil, remove from the heat and place the stainless steel bowl on top, making sure the base of the bowl does not touch the water. Slowly melt the chocolate off the heat — it should take 10 minutes and will need to be stirred occasionally.

Meanwhile, put the remaining cream in a bowl and whip until soft peaks form, being careful not to overbeat. Refrigerate until needed.

Place the egg yolks in a stainless steel bowl and pour the sugar for the yolks on top and whisk well. Place over a saucepan of simmering water, making sure the base of the bowl does not touch the water. Whisk continuously for 2–3 minutes, or until the yolks are light and foamy. When you lift the whisk out of the mixture and let some fall back into the bowl it should sit on top for a few seconds before disappearing back into the mix. Remove from the heat.

Whisk the egg whites in a clean bowl until foamy, then sprinkle in the sugar for the whites, whisking continuously until soft peaks form.

Remove the cream from the refrigerator and if it has become runny, whisk it until soft peaks form. Add 3 tablespoons of whipped cream to the melted chocolate. Whisk the warm egg yolk mixture into the warm chocolate to combine — it is important that they are both warm or the mix will cease (if the chocolate has cooled you will need to gently reheat it). Fold the egg white mixture into the remaining whipped cream, then fold this into the chocolate mix until well combined. Cover with plastic wrap and refrigerate overnight to set.

To make the raspberry purée, put the raspberries and sugar in a food processor and process until smooth. Transfer to a bowl, cover with plastic wrap and refrigerate until needed.

Follow the instructions on pages 152–7 to roll out the pastry and use it to line twenty 8 cm (3¼ inch) round fluted loose-based tart tins. Set the pastry cases in the freezer for at least 20 minutes.

Blind bake the tart cases in a preheated 200°C (400°F/Gas 6) oven for 20–25 minutes, or until golden. Remove from the oven and allow to cool.

To assemble the tarts, spoon about ¾ teaspoon of raspberry purée into the base of each tart shell. Place the mousse in a piping (icing) bag fitted with a plain nozzle and pipe into the tart shells to slightly overfill them. With a small palette knife, scrape the mousse to be flush with the top of the tart shell. Sprinkle the chocolate cake crumbs over the top of each tart and serve.

ingredients

strawberry purée

250 g (9 oz/1²⁄₃ cups) strawberries, washed
and hulled

120 g (4¹⁄₄ oz) caster (superfine) sugar

crème brûlée custard

720 ml (25 fl oz) pouring (whipping) cream (35% fat)

1 vanilla bean, split lengthways

10 egg yolks

80 g (2³⁄₄ oz/¹⁄₃ cup) caster (superfine) sugar,
plus extra for burning

1 quantity sweet shortcrust pastry (see pages 152–7)

It is not uncommon to be served a classic vanilla brûlée in a restaurant with fresh strawberries served on the side. This version is the classic brûlée piped into a tart shell with strawberry purée in the bottom containing the whole dessert in a neat and edible package. If you prefer, you can bake the custard on its own in ramekins and caramelise the top to make a classic crème brûlée. Much the same as the ginger brûlée tarts, this filling can be tricky to get right.

vanilla brûlée tarts with strawberry purée

makes 20

method

To make the strawberry purée, put the strawberries and sugar in a food processor and process until smooth. Transfer to a bowl, cover with plastic wrap and refrigerate until needed.

To make the crème brûlée custard, put the cream into a saucepan, scrape the seeds of the vanilla bean into the cream and add the bean. Bring to the boil over high heat. As soon as it boils, remove from the heat and set aside for about 10 minutes.

Place the egg yolks in a stainless steel bowl and use a whisk to combine. Add the sugar and continue whisking for about 30 seconds, or until the sugar has dissolved. Pour the slightly cooled cream through a fine sieve, discarding the vanilla bean, then pour the cream into the egg yolk mixture, stirring well to combine.

Put the bowl over a saucepan of simmering water, making sure the base of the bowl does not touch the water, and continue stirring with a whisk for about 10–15 minutes, or until the mixture is smooth and thick, scraping down the sides of the bowl regularly with a rubber spatula. It is important to keep stirring at all times or the mixture will curdle. Remove the bowl from the heat and whisk briskly for about 2 minutes to cool it quickly. Over the next 1 hour, whisk the mixture every 10 minutes until cooled. Use a rubber spatula to clean the side of the bowl thoroughly and place plastic wrap directly on top of the mixture; refrigerate overnight to set.

Follow the instructions on pages 152–7 to roll out the pastry and use it to line twenty 8 cm (3¼ inch) round fluted loose-based tart tins. Set the pastry cases in the freezer for at least 20 minutes.

Blind bake the tart cases in a preheated 200°C (400°F/Gas 6) oven for 20–25 minutes, or until golden. Remove from the oven and allow to cool.

To assemble the tarts, spoon about ¾ teaspoon of strawberry purée in the centre of the base of each tart shell. Pipe custard into the tart shells with a piping (icing) bag fitted with a plain nozzle — you should just slightly overfill the filling in each one. With a small palette knife, scrape the custard to be flush with the top of the tart shell. Place in the refrigerator for 4 hours.

Sprinkle 1 teaspoon caster sugar onto the top of the custard and burn with a blowtorch until it caramelises If you don't have a blowtorch the tarts are still very tasty without the extra sugar and burning.

variation

To make classic créme brûlées, preheat the oven to 140°C (275°F/Gas 1). Use the recipe and method above for making the crème brûlée custard, but after mixing the cream into the yolk mix, pour the warm custard into ten ½-cup ramekins, until full. Place the ramekins in a deep baking tray and pour in enough water to come halfway up the sides of the ramekins. Cook in the oven for 45 minutes, or until just set. Remove from the oven and allow to cool, then place in the refrigerator for at least 4 hours. Sprinkle 2 teaspoons caster sugar over the top of each ramekin and burn the top with a blowtorch until it caramelises.

ingredients

crème pâtissière

250 ml (9 fl oz/1 cup) milk

1 vanilla bean, split lengthways

50 g (1³/₄ oz) caster (superfine) sugar

3 egg yolks

15 g (½ oz) plain (all-purpose) flour

frangipane

170 g (6 oz/³/₄ cup) caster (superfine) sugar

170 g (6 oz) unsalted butter

3 eggs

280 g (10 oz/2³/₄ cups) ground almonds

60 ml (2 fl oz/¼ cup) Grand Marnier

1 quantity sweet shortcrust pastry (see pages 152–7)

20 poached pears wedges (see page 188), halved

pear and almond tarts

makes 20

This tart uses poached pears but you can use roasted rhubarb or plum from page 184. The frangipane can be used without the addition of crème pâtissière, but we believe the addition provides moisture and makes the result less cake-like. You can substitute finely ground hazelnuts or pistachios for the ground almonds if you wish.

method

To make the crème pâtissière, pour the milk into a saucepan and scrape in the vanilla seeds and bean. Heat up until just below boiling point, then remove from the heat and pour into a container to cool completely. Refrigerate for at least 6 hours to allow the vanilla to infuse.

Gently reheat the milk over low heat. Put the egg yolks in a stainless steel bowl and whisk continuously, adding the sugar a little at a time until completely combined. Continue whisking while adding the flour until the mixture is completely smooth. Pour the warm milk through a fine sieve directly onto the egg yolk mixture and whisk well until smooth and combined. Return this custard to a clean saucepan and bring to the boil, stirring continuously with a wooden spoon. Once the custard boils, reduce the heat and simmer for a further 5 minutes, stirring continuously. Remove from the heat, allow to cool, then transfer to an airtight container. Place plastic wrap directly on the surface of the custard, cover with a lid and refrigerate until ready to use. The crème pâtissière can be made in advance and stored for 3 days.

To make the frangipane, put the sugar and butter in the bowl of an electric mixer fitted with a paddle attachment. Mix on low speed until pale and creamy. Add the eggs, one at a time, making sure each is well combined before adding more. Add the ground almonds and mix on low speed until combined, then add the Grand Marnier until completely incorporated. Set aside until needed.

Follow the instructions on pages 152–7 to roll out the pastry and use it to line twenty 8 cm (3¼ inch) round fluted loose-baseed tart tins. Set the pastry cases in the freezer for at least 20 minutes.

Blind bake the tart cases in a preheated 200°C (400°F/Gas 6) oven for 20–25 minutes, or until golden. Remove from the oven and allow to cool.

Lower the oven temperature to 190°C (375°F/Gas 5). To assemble the tarts, fold the frangipane and crème pâtissière together until completely combined, then spoon 2 tablespoons into each of the pastry cases. Arrange the pears in the top of the tarts in a decorative pattern and bake for 20 minutes, or until golden.

ingredients

1 quantity sweet shortcrust pastry (see pages 152–7)

1 kg (2 lb 4 oz oz/4 cups) ricotta cheese

100 g (3½ oz) icing (confectioners') sugar, sifted

1 vanilla bean, split lengthways

1 kg (2 lb 4 oz) strawberries, rinsed, hulled and quartered

We rarely make these tarts at the Bakery due to their extremely short shelf-life. Although we assemble tarts three or four times daily, we realised this one was best eaten within 2 hours of being assembled, which is a shame, as it is so simple and perfect. The ricotta for this recipe needs to be quite dry. If the ricotta you have is soft and wet, leave it to drain overnight in the refrigerator in a sieve lined with a clean tea towel (dish towel). Figs also work particularly well in these tarts during the autumn months when they are available perfectly ripe. The ricotta filling can also be dolloped onto a plate with fresh fruit for a simple but fresh summer dessert.

strawberry and ricotta tarts

makes 20

method

Follow the instructions on pages 152–7 to roll out the pastry and use it to line twenty 8 cm (3¼ inch) round fluted loose-based tart tins. Set the pastry cases in the freezer for at least 20 minutes.

Blind bake the tart cases in a preheated 200°C (400°F/Gas 6) oven for 20–25 minutes, or until golden. Remove from the oven and allow to cool.

To make the filling, put the ricotta in a food processor with the icing sugar and scrape in the vanilla seeds, discarding the bean. Process until smooth and well combined.

Pipe about 2 tablespoons of the ricotta filling into each tart shell until full to the brim. Arrange the strawberries on top and serve immediately.

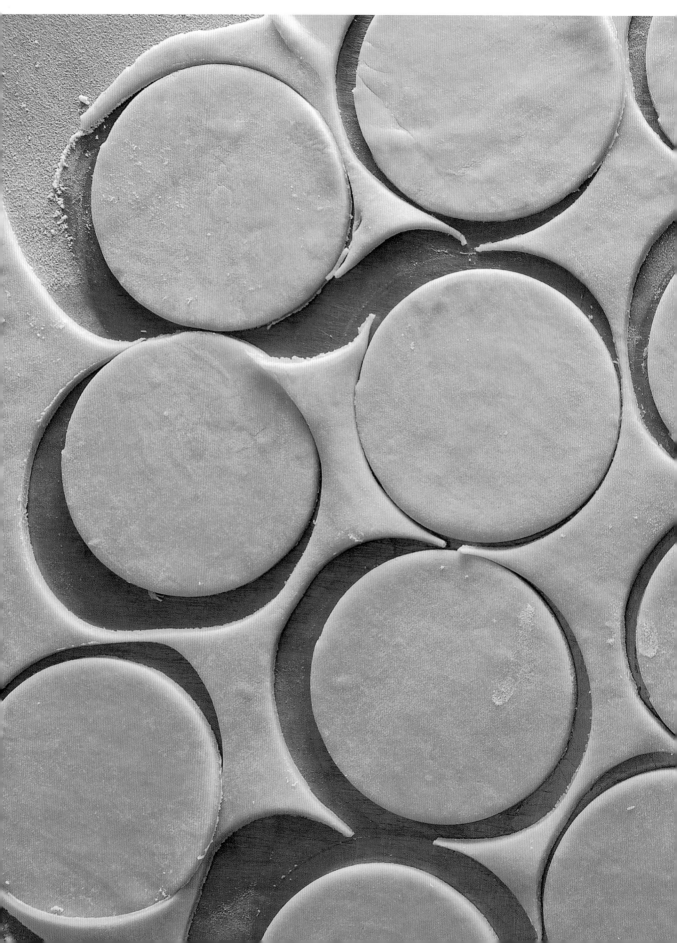

ingredients
1 quantity sweet shortcrust pastry (see pages 152–7)

30 pitted prunes, cut into thirds

80 ml (2½ fl oz/⅓ cup) brandy

egg wash

2 egg yolks

25 ml (¾ fl oz) pouring (whipping) cream (35% fat)

custard

5 egg yolks

45 g (1¾ oz) caster (superfine) sugar

415 ml (14¼ fl oz) pouring (whipping) cream (35% fat)

1 vanilla bean, split lengthways

custard tarts with prunes makes 20

These are delicious tarts adapted from a classic prune and Armagnac tart from France. They work beautifully with any stone fruits in summer and equally well with dried fruits plumped in alcohol. The poached pears on page 188 will also work very well in this recipe.

This tart requires a bit of effort and can be tricky to get right, but if you would like a recipe in your repertoire that will earn you the greatest compliments every time you bake it, this is one to perfect. The difficulty with this recipe is to produce egg yolk custard without it curdling. You are looking for a fairly high ratio of fruit to custard, pouring a small pool of custard around fruit protruding from the tart. Bake the tarts on the top shelf of the oven and if your oven has the option to heat both the top and bottom, set the top element on high. The temperatures given are approximate, and more than any other recipe in this book, you will need to find the temperature and timing that works for your oven. Make sure you keep note of your cooking times and temperatures so that when you get it right, you can repeat it again and again.

method

Put the prunes in a bowl and pour over the brandy. Cover with plastic wrap and set aside for 24 hours to soak.

Follow the instructions on pages 152–7 to roll out the pastry and use it to line twenty 8 cm (3¼ inch) round fluted loose-based tart tins. Set the pastry cases in the freezer for at least 20 minutes.

Blind bake the tart cases in a preheated 200°C (400°F/Gas 6) oven for 20–25 minutes, or until golden. Remove from the oven and allow to cool.

Make the egg wash by mixing the egg yolks and cream together in a bowl until well combined. Brush the egg mixture on the base and sides of the tart shells and bake for about 4 minutes to seal the shells — the shells are sealed when the egg wash has dried into a shiny glaze. This will stop the custard soaking into the shells resulting in an unappealing soggy shell.

Place 4 or 5 pieces of drained prune in the base of each pastry shell. Reduce the oven temperature to 180°C (350°F/Gas 4).

To make the custard, put the egg yolks and sugar into the bowl of an electric mixer fitted with a whisk attachment. Scrape the vanilla seeds into the bowl and mix on medium speed for about 1 minute, or until combined. Remove the egg yolks from the mixer, pour in the cream and stir in by hand using a whisk. Set aside for 30 minutes.

Pour the custard mixture over the prunes in the pastry shells and fill to the brim. Slide onto the top shelf of the oven and bake for about 5 minutes — at this stage the tarts will be slightly golden on top and just starting to set. Gently shake the baking tray, the custard should be starting to firm around the edge of the tart shell. The custard must not boil, if it boils it will spoil the texture. Reduce the oven temperature to 110°C (225°F/Gas ½) and open the door, holding it ajar with the help of a wooden spoon if needed. Leave the tarts to cook for a further 20 minutes in the cooling oven. Check the custard has set by giving the tray a light shake.

These tarts are best eaten about 2 hours after baking, once they have reached room temperature.

ingredients

1 quantity sweet shortcrust pastry (see pages 152–7)

vanilla and lime pannacotta

400 ml (14 fl oz) pouring (whipping) cream (35% fat)

200 ml (7 fl oz) full cream (whole) milk

120 g (4¼ oz) caster (superfine) sugar

½ vanilla bean, split lengthways

finely grated zest of 2 limes

2 x 2 g (¹⁄₁₆ oz) gelatine leaves or 1 teaspoon gelatine powder

1 tablespoon freshly squeezed lime juice

1 tablespoon water

lime jelly

320 ml (11 fl oz) freshly squeezed lime juice

80 ml (2½ fl oz/⅓ cup) water

80 g (2¾ oz/⅓ cup) caster (superfine) sugar

6 x 2 g (¹⁄₁₆ oz) gelatine leaves or 3 teaspoons gelatine powder

vanilla and lime pannacotta tart

makes 20

Pannacotta is one of the simplest desserts to make. It is a jelly based on milk and cream, and basically all that you are doing is warming the ingredients then setting them with gelatine. The vanilla cream in this tart, with a hint of lime in the background, tastes delicious. The tart is topped with a thin layer of lime jelly, enhancing the lime flavour, and adding an appealing shine to the top of the tart.

method

Follow the instructions on pages 152–7 to roll out the pastry and use it to line twenty 8 cm (3¼ inch) round fluted loose-based tart tins. Set the pastry cases in the freezer for at least 20 minutes.

Blind bake the tart cases in a preheated 200°C (400°F/Gas 6) oven for 20–25 minutes, or until golden. Remove from the oven and allow to cool.

To make the pannacotta, put the cream, milk and sugar in a saucepan over medium heat. Scrape the seeds from the vanilla bean into the pan and add the bean. Stir for about 2 minutes, or until the sugar dissolves, then remove from the heat just before the mixture boils. Stir in the lime zest. If using gelatine leaves, soak them in 1 litre (35 fl oz/4 cups) cold water for about 2 minutes to soften, then squeeze to remove the excess water. Stir into the cream mixture with the lime juice and water. If using powdered gelatine, put the gelatine in a saucepan over low heat with the lime juice and water, stir to dissolve the gelatine, then stir into the cream mixture. Allow to cool to room temperature, about 1 hour.

Pour the cream mixture through a fine sieve to remove the vanilla bean and lime zest, then carefully pour into the tart shells, filling them to three-quarters full. Place in the refrigerator to fully set, about 2 hours.

While the pannacotta is setting, make the lime jelly. Put the lime juice, water and sugar in a small saucepan over medium heat and bring just to the boil. Remove from the heat. If using gelatine leaves, soak them in 1 litre (35 fl oz/ 4 cups) cold water for about 2 minutes to soften, then squeeze to remove the excess water. Stir into the lime juice mix. If using powdered gelatine, mix in a bowl with the water and 2 tablespoons lime juice, stirring well. Put the remaining lime juice and sugar in a small saucepan over medium heat and bring just to the boil. Remove from the heat and stir in the gelatine mix to dissolve.

Allow the lime jelly to cool to room temperature, then carefully spoon 1–2 tablespoons of the jelly over the pannacotta in each tart shell — the pannacotta mix must be completely set at this stage or the jelly will pour straight through it. Take care not to damage the smooth top of the pannacotta while spooning over the jelly. Place back in the refrigerator for 1 hour to set.

variation

This pannacotta can also be made in ramekins and served as a dessert if you wish. This recipe yields enough for about six 100 ml (3½ fl oz) ramekins. Simply pour the jelly into the moulds, allow to set, then pour over the pannacotta and refrigerate until set.

ingredients

Italian meringue

200 g (7 oz) caster (superfine) sugar, plus 20 g (³⁄₄ oz) extra

100 ml (3¹⁄₂ fl oz) water

4 egg whites

passionfruit bavarois

300 ml (10¹⁄₂ fl oz) milk

3 x 2 g (¹⁄₁₆ oz) gelatine leaves or 2 teaspoons gelatine powder

6 egg yolks

175 g (6 oz) caster (superfine) sugar

250 ml (9 fl oz/1 cup) passionfruit juice (see note, page 291)

350 ml (12 fl oz) pouring (whipping) cream (35% fat)

1 quantity sweet shortcrust pastry (see pages 152–7)

This tart is filled with a bavarois mix, which is really just a mousse without the egg whites. The soft meringue is an Italian meringue where a hot sugar syrup is whisked into the egg whites and effectively cooks the whites during the mixing stage. You will need a sugar thermometer to measure the temperature of the sugar syrup. After mixing, no further cooking is required, however the meringues are usually browned quickly with a blowtorch before serving.

passionfruit tarts with soft meringue makes 20

method

Follow the instructions on pages 152–7 to roll out the pastry and use it to line twenty 8 cm (3¹⁄₄ inch) round fluted loose-based tart tins. Set the pastry cases in the freezer for at least 20 minutes.

Blind bake the tart cases in a preheated 200°C (400°F/Gas 6) oven for 20–25 minutes, or until golden. Remove from the oven and allow to cool.

To make the pasionfruit bavarois, put the milk in a saucepan over high heat and bring to just boiling. Soften the gelatine leaves in 1 litre (35 fl oz/4 cups) cold water. If using powdered gelatine, mix in a bowl with 2 tablespoons of the milk. Put the remaining milk in a saucepan over high heat and bring to just boiling.

Whisk the egg yolks, sugar and passionfruit together in a stainless steel bowl. Sit the bowl over a saucepan of simmering water, making sure the base of the bowl does not touch the water. Add the hot milk and continue whisking for about 5 minutes, or until the mixture is quite thick. Squeeze the excess water from the gelatine leaves and whisk into the passionfruit mixture. If using powdered gelatine, whisk the gelatine mixture into the passionfruit mixture. Pour through a fine sieve and refrigerate for 30 minutes to 1 hour, or until it is just starting to set. Any leftover filling can be poured into ramekins or similar serving dishes and eaten as a dessert.

Whip the cream to soft peaks, then fold through the passionfruit mixture, taking care not to overwhip the cream or it will not fold through easily. Pour the bavarois carefully into the pastry shells, filling them to the brim. Place in the refrigerator for 2–3 hours, or until set.

While the passionfruit bavarois is setting, make the Italian meringue. You will need a sugar thermometer to successfully make this recipe. Have a glass of cold water and a pastry brush ready to brush down the sides of the saucepan to stop sugar crystals forming.

Put the sugar and water in a small heavy-based saucepan over high heat. Bring to the boil, stirring until the mixture boils, then stop stirring, as this will cause sugar crystals to form. Brush the sides of the saucepan with a wet pastry brush every couple of minutes or when you see crystals starting to form. Allow the mixture to keep boiling until it reaches 118°C (244°F) on the thermometer, then remove from the heat immediately.

Put the egg whites in a very clean bowl of an electric mixer fitted with a whisk attachment. Mix on high speed for about 2 minutes, or until foamy, then add the extra sugar and whisk until soft peaks form. With the mixer still running on high, slowly pour the sugar syrup into the whites, adding small amounts at a time and making sure it is incorporated before adding more. Take care not to pour the syrup directly onto the beater to avoid spraying boiling syrup over yourself. Once all the syrup is added, turn the mixer to low speed and keep mixing for a further 10–15 minutes, or until the meringue is cool.

To assemble the tarts, use a piping (icing) bag to pipe the meringue onto the top of the bavarois, completely covering the top of the tart — then use a palette knife to create a less formal shape. Brown the meringue with a blowtorch or place it under a very hot grill (broiler) for 30–45 seconds, or until browned — make sure you watch it carefully as it will burn very quickly.

note

Make the passionfruit juice by straining passionfruit pulp into a bowl, scraping and forcing it through a sieve with the back of a spoon — you should need 10–15 passionfruit to make 1 cup juice, depending on the fruit.

1 quantity sweet shortcrust pastry (see pages 152–7)

750 g (1 lb 10 oz/3 cups) crème pâtissière

(see pages 276–7 — you will need to triple this recipe)

20 ml (½ fl oz/1 tablespoon) Grand Marnier

80 ml (2½ fl oz/⅓ cup) pouring (whipping) cream (35% fat)

250 g (9 oz) strawberries, washed, hulled and halved

125 g (4½ oz) raspberries, washed

125 g (4½ oz) blueberries, washed

125 g (4½ oz) blackberries, washed

This is a delicious tart that makes a great barbecue-lunch dessert. It is best assembled at the last minute to ensure the crispest possible pastry shell. The custard should be silky smooth and the berries of the best quality and perfectly ripe.

summer berry custard tarts
makes 20

method

Follow the instructions on pages 152–7 to roll out the pastry and use it to line twenty 8 cm (3¼ inch) round fluted loose-based tart tins. Set the pastry cases in the freezer for at least 20 minutes.

Blind bake the tart cases in a preheated 200°C (400°F/Gas 6) oven for 20–25 minutes, or until golden. Remove from the oven and allow to cool.

Put the crème pâttisiére and Grand Marnier in the bowl of an electric mixer fitted with a whisk attachment. Mix on high speed until smooth. Whip the cream to soft peaks. Fold the whipped cream through the crème pâtissière mixture and place in the refrigerator for 1 hour to chill.

Spoon about 2 tablespoons of the custard mixture into each tart shell and arrange the mixed berries on top. Serve immediately.

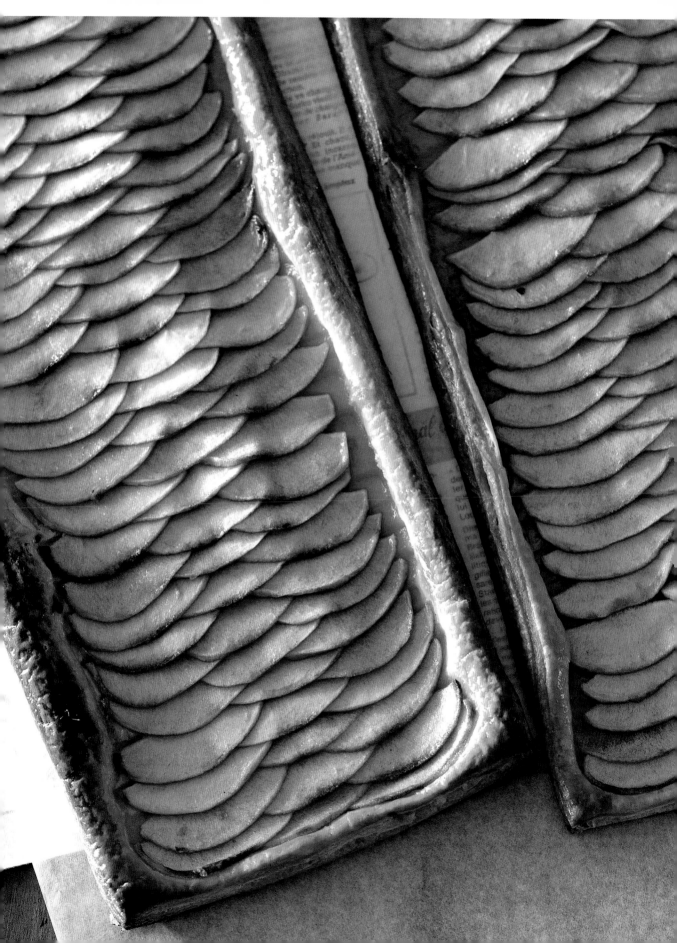

ingredients

4 granny smith apples
200 g (7 oz) soft brown sugar
4 lemons
½ quantity puff pastry (see pages 162–5)
125 g (4½ oz/½ cup) crème pâtissière (see pages 276–7)
egg wash (see page 168), for brushing

We make this apple galette with puff pastry, but you can make it with croissant dough. The apples are sliced quite thinly, macerated overnight and layered over the pastry with crème pâtissière. It is then baked in a hot oven to tinge the edges of the apples a deep caramel colour. The pastry needs to be very dark and crisp, so don't be afraid of leaving it in the oven 3–4 minutes longer when you think it's cooked. You will need to prepare the apples a day in advance.

apple galette serves 6

method

Peel the apples and remove the cheeks from each side of the cores, then remove the two remaining half moons from each core. Slice the apple pieces into 2 mm (¹⁄₁₆ inch) slices and re-form into the original cheek shape. Place the apples in formation in a square or rectangular container that will fit them snugly. Pack the sugar over the top. Finely grate the zest of the lemons. Squeeze the juice of the lemons into a bowl and stir in the zest, then pour this over the sugar. Cover with plastic wrap and refrigerate overnight.

Preheat the oven to its highest temperature. Roll out the puff pastry and cut into a rectangle, about 17 x 30 cm (6½ x 12 inches) and 3 mm (⅛ inch) thick. Place the pastry on a baking tray lined with baking paper. Spread the crème pâtissière over the pastry, leaving a 1 cm (½ inch) border around the edges.

Drain the apples well by gently squeezing out any liquid and arrange them over the top of the pastry so they slightly overlap, leaving a border around the edge. Brush the exposed pastry edges with a little egg wash and cook in the oven for 12–15 minutes, or until a deep caramel colour. Cool on the tray before slicing and serving.

more sweets

cakes
and biscuits

The cakes, biscuits and muffins we make at Bourke Street Bakery have a naturally rustic home-made look and are made to have a fine texture and flavour. They are the type of cake you can enjoy any time of day when you're in need of a sweet hit. The cakes in this chapter are suitable for morning or afternoon tea, make an unforgettable late-night supper or can be dressed up with some fruit, cream or a sweet sauce to make a decadent dessert.

ingredients

70 g (2$\frac{1}{2}$ oz) walnuts

150 g (5$\frac{1}{2}$ oz/1 cup) self-raising flour

$\frac{1}{8}$ teaspoon baking powder

$\frac{1}{8}$ teaspoon bicarbonate of soda (baking soda)

$\frac{1}{4}$ teaspoon ground cinnamon

$\frac{1}{8}$ teaspoon ground cloves

$\frac{1}{8}$ teaspoon ground nutmeg

$\frac{1}{4}$ teaspoon salt

55 ml (1$\frac{3}{4}$ fl oz/about 2) egg whites

60 g (2$\frac{1}{4}$ oz/$\frac{1}{4}$ cup) sugar for egg whites

1 egg

1 egg yolk

160 g (5$\frac{3}{4}$ oz/$\frac{3}{4}$ cup) sugar for egg yolks

170 ml (5$\frac{1}{2}$ fl oz/$\frac{2}{3}$ cup) extra light olive oil

125 g (4$\frac{1}{2}$ oz) carrots, peeled and grated

cream cheese frosting

20 g ($\frac{3}{4}$ oz/1 tablespoon) icing (confectioners') sugar, plus extra, for dusting

20 g ($\frac{3}{4}$ oz/1 tablespoon) butter, softened

145 g (5$\frac{1}{4}$ oz) cream cheese (preferably Neufchâtel)

40 ml (1$\frac{1}{4}$ fl oz/2 tablespoons) pouring (whipping) cream (35% fat)

carrot cake

serves 10

It is necessary to work quickly to make this recipe succeed. Everything is whipped to incorporate a lot of air and the dry ingredients are quickly folded through at the end. The whipped egg whites result in a fantastic crisp meringue-like top on the cake. We have a number of mixers, so we can have everything mixing at one time, but for a home kitchen you will get the best results working in the order listed within the recipe.

method

Preheat the oven to 200°C (400°F/Gas 6). Grease an 18 cm (7 inch) round cake tin and line the base and side with baking paper — the paper should protrude about 2.5 cm (1 inch) above the tin.

Place the walnuts on a baking tray and cook for 4–5 minutes, or until lightly roasted. Cool and cut into thirds. Sift the flour, baking powder, bicarbonate of soda, spices and salt into a bowl. Repeat to ensure they are evenly mixed.

Put the egg whites in a very clean bowl of an electric mixer fitted with a whisk attachment. Beat the egg whites on high speed until soft peaks start to form. Slowly pour in the sugar for the egg whites, while the motor is still running, being careful not to overmix — the meringue should reach soft peak stage. Quickly transfer the meringue to another bowl and set aside until needed.

Put the egg and egg yolk in the bowl of the electric mixer and add the sugar for the egg yolks. Mix on high speed for 3–4 minutes, or until the mixture doubles in volume and is quite airy. With the motor still running, slowly pour in the oil in a thin stream being careful that it doesn't split or deflate too much.

Remove the bowl from the mixer and with a spatula or gloved hand, gently fold in the flour mixture until combined. Fold in the carrots and walnuts. Quickly and lightly fold in the meringue — do not fold it through completely, you should still be able to see streaks of meringue through the mix. Pour into the prepared tin and bake for 1 hour 10 minutes, or until a skewer inserted into the centre of the cake comes out clean. You may need to drop the oven temperature to 180°C (350°F/Gas 4) after the first 30 minutes if the top is browning too quickly.

Meanwhile, make the cream cheese frosting. Cream the icing sugar and butter in the bowl of an electric mixer until pale and smooth. Add the cream cheese in small amounts, allowing it to be completely incorporated before adding the rest. Scrape down the sides of the mixing bowl during this process to ensure even mixing. Add the cream and mix until smooth, being careful not to overmix at this stage or the cream may curdle and separate. If using a different type of cream cheese for this recipe you may need to add a little more cream — the frosting needs to be of a spreadable consistency but not at all runny.

Remove the cake from the oven and allow to cool in the tin for about 30 minutes before turning it out onto a wire rack to cool completely. Using a serrated knife, slice horizontally through the centre of the cake to form two even-sized layers and fill with cream cheese frosting. Dust the top of the cake with icing sugar to serve.

ingredients

165 g (5¾ oz/1⅔ cups) rolled (porridge) oats

220 g (7¾ oz) plain (all-purpose) flour

100 g (3½ oz) desiccated coconut

210 g (7½ oz) soft brown sugar

50 g (1¾ oz) dried barberries

45 ml (1½ fl oz) boiling water

185 g (6½ oz) unsalted butter

60 g (2¼ oz) golden syrup or honey

1½ teaspoons bicarbonate of soda (baking soda)

60 ml (2 fl oz/¼ cup) water

This recipe is based on the Anzac biscuit with the addition of dried barberries that have been plumped up in hot water and brown sugar. A barberry is a small red berry similar to a red currant, and is often used in Middle Eastern cuisines; it has a slightly acidic flavour. At the Bakery, we press the biscuits down to make them very thin.

oat and barberry biscuits

makes 12

method

Preheat the oven to 170°C (325°F/Gas 3).

Put the oats, flour, coconut and 175 g (6 oz) of the sugar into a bowl and mix well to combine.

Put the barberries in a bowl with the remaining sugar and pour in the boiling water, stirring a little to dissolve the sugar.

Put the butter and golden syrup in a saucepan over low heat and stir until the butter has melted. Add the barberries and syrup. Remove from the heat. Combine the bicarbonate of soda with the water and stir into the pan. Pour the wet ingredients onto the dry ingredients while still foaming and mix together with a large spoon.

Take 3 tablespoons of the mixture at a time and roll into even-sized balls — you should make about 12 balls in total. Place the balls on baking trays lined with baking paper and press down using a thin metal spatula to make very thin rounds. Bake the biscuits, in batches, for 15–20 minutes each. Remove from the oven and allow to cool on the trays. These biscuits can be stored for up to 1 week in an airtight container.

ingredients

2 eggs

150 ml (5 fl oz) buttermilk

125 g (4½ oz) plain (all-purpose) flour

40 g (1½ oz) potato flour

½ teaspoon baking powder

⅛ teaspoon bicarbonate of soda (baking soda)

65 g (2½ oz) unsweetened cocoa powder

¼ teaspoon salt

280 g (10 oz/1¼ cups) caster (superfine) sugar

110 g (3¾ oz) unsalted butter, cut into 3 cm (1¼ inch) cubes, softened

1¼ cups chocolate mousse, for filling (see page 268–9)

raspberries, to serve

icing (confectioners') sugar, for dusting

chocolate cake serves 10

method

Preheat the oven to 180°C (350°F/Gas 4). Grease two 20 cm (8 inch) round sponge cake tins and line the base and side with baking paper.

Put the eggs and buttermilk in a bowl and whisk together until well combined. Set aside until needed.

Sift the plain flour, potato flour, baking powder, bicarbonate of soda, cocoa powder and salt into the bowl of an electric mixer fitted with a paddle attachment. Add the sugar and butter and mix on low speed for about 1 minute, or until the butter is incorporated. Increase the speed to medium and add the buttermilk mixture in three batches, mixing for about 30 seconds between each batch and scraping down the sides after each addition. Divide evenly between the two cake tins and bake for 20–25 minutes, or until a skewer inserted into the centre of the cakes comes out clean. Allow the cakes to cool for 10 minutes in the tin before turning out onto a wire rack to cool completely. Decorate with raspberries and dust with icing sugar to serve.

note

You can make crumbs from one of these cakes that are used in the chocolate mousse tarts on pages 268–9. Simply cut one of the cooled cakes into 3 cm (1¼ inch) pieces. Place on a baking tray and cook in a 150°C (300°F/Gas 2) oven for about 30 minutes, or until dry. Place in a food processor a little at a time, and pulse to form coarse crumbs. Place on a tray and cook in the oven for 30 minutes longer, or until dry, then pulse again in a food processor. Cool and store in an airtight container for up to 5 days.

ingredients

250 g (9 oz) unsalted butter

355 g (12½ oz) caster (superfine) sugar

1 vanilla bean, seeds scraped

4 eggs

200 g (7 oz) sour cream

300 g (10½ oz/2 cups) self-raising flour, sifted

24 poached pear wedges (see page 188)

125 g (4½ oz/1 cup) fresh raspberries

This is a versatile cake — at Bourke Street Bakery, we put the batter in the cake tin first and the fruit on top. The fruit sinks into the cake as it bakes and ends up on the bottom of the tin. The cake is then inverted to serve.

sour cream butter cake with pears and raspberries serves 16

method

Preheat the oven to 200°C (400°F/Gas 6). Grease a 28 cm (11¼ inch) round cake tin and line the base and side with baking paper — the paper should protrude about 2.5 cm (1 inch) above the tin.

Put the butter, sugar and vanilla seeds in the bowl of an electric mixer fitted with a whisk attachment. Whisk on low speed until pale and creamy. Add the eggs one at a time, making sure they are completely incorporated before adding more. Add the sour cream in two batches, then add the flour in two batches, until well combined. Using a rubber spatula, scoop the mixture into the prepared cake tin. Arrange the pear wedges in an even circle around the tin, then scatter the raspberries over the top. Bake for 55 minutes to 1 hour 15 minutes, or until a skewer comes out clean when inserted into the centre of the cake. Cover the top of the cake loosely with baking paper if it starts to brown. Remove from the oven and allow to cool in the tin for 10 minutes before turning out onto a wire rack to cool completely. This cake is best eaten as soon as it has cooled but can be stored in an airtight container for up to 3 days.

variation

Different fruits sink to different degrees and it is also possible to pour the batter over the top of the fruit in the tin. Basically, any fresh fruit will work as long as it's not too watery, or if it's a hard fruit, it should first be poached. You can also omit the fruit and make a plain sour cream cake instead, or add 2 tablespoons of poppy seeds and the finely grated zest of 2 lemons.

ingredients

7 eggs, at room temperature

175 g (6 oz/¾ cup) caster (superfine) sugar

60 g (2¼ oz) unsalted butter

170 g (6 oz) plain (all-purpose) flour

200 ml (7 fl oz) pouring (whipping) cream (35% fat), whipped

200 g (7 oz) raspberry jam

icing (confectioners') sugar, for dusting

sponge cake

serves 10

method

Preheat the oven to 190°C (375°F/Gas 5). Grease two 20 cm (8 inch) round sponge cake tins and line the base and side with baking paper — the paper should protrude about 2.5 cm (1 inch) above the tins.

Break the eggs into the bowl of an electric mixer fitted with a whisk attachment. Add the sugar and mix on high speed for 4–5 minutes, or until nearly tripled in volume. While the eggs are whisking melt the butter and sift the flour 3 times.

Remove the bowl of whipped eggs from the electric mixer and using a hand-held whisk, fold through about half of the sifted flour — about six or seven deft strokes with the whisk should be enough. Add the rest of the flour and fold through quickly, trying not to knock too much air out of the mixture. Fold through the melted butter, again trying not to knock too much air out of the mixture.

Pour the mixture into the prepared tins. Bake for 25–30 minutes, or until the cake springs back when gently pressed with your finger. Each cake will also start to shrink away from the side of its tin when it is cooked. Remove the cakes from the oven and allow to cool in the tins for 10 minutes before turning out onto a wire rack to cool completely.

Once cooled, spread the cream over one of the cakes and top with jam, then sandwich the two cakes together and dust the top with icing sugar.

ingredients

235 g (8½ oz) dark chocolate
(55% cocoa), chopped

150 g (5½ oz/1 cup) plain
(all-purpose) flour

40 g (1½ oz/⅓ cup) unsweetened
cocoa powder

1½ teaspoons bicarbonate of
soda (baking soda)

½ teaspoon salt

100 g (3½ oz) unsalted butter

240 g (8¾ oz) soft brown sugar

2 eggs

85 g (3 oz) dried sour cherries

This is a super-rich chocolate biscuit that, when baked to perfection, is crisp on the outside and fudge-like in the centre. The slight acidity of the occasional dried sour cherry cuts through the richness. The cherries can be replaced with other dried fruit or a mix of fruit and nuts if you prefer.

chocolate sour cherry biscuits

makes 12

method

Preheat the oven to 165°C (320°F/Gas 3).

Put the chocolate in a large stainless steel bowl and set over a saucepan of simmering water, making sure the base of the bowl does not touch the water. Allow the water in the saucepan to boil for 2 minutes, then turn off the heat and stir the chocolate while it slowly melts.

Sift the flour, cocoa powder, bicarbonate of soda and salt into a bowl.

Put the butter and sugar in the bowl of an electric mixer fitted with a whisk attachment. Whisk on medium speed until pale and creamy. Add the eggs, one at a time, making sure each is incorporated before adding more. Add the dry ingredients in three batches, mixing well after each addition, then add the melted chocolate and mix until well combined.

Remove the bowl from the mixer, then fold through the dried sour cherries. The mix can become quite sticky, so you may need to refrigerate it for 15 minutes before shaping the biscuits. Take 3 tablespoons of mixture at a time and roll into even-sized balls — you should make about 12 balls in total. Place the balls on baking trays lined with baking paper, allowing room for them to spread. Refrigerate for a further 30 minutes, or until firm. Bake in batches, for 15–20 minutes each, or until risen and quite cracked on top. Cool on the trays and eat, or store in an airtight container for up to 3 days.

ingredients

banana cake

250 g (9 oz) unsalted butter

355 g (12½ oz) caster (superfine) sugar

1 vanilla bean, split lengthways

4 eggs

200 g (7 oz) sour cream

300 g (10½ oz/2 cups) self-raising flour, sifted

2–3 ripe bananas

20 g (¾ oz) golden syrup or soft brown sugar

caramel sauce

200 ml (7 fl oz) pouring (whipping) cream (35% fat)

100 ml (3½ fl oz) water

300 g (10½ oz) caster (superfine) sugar

30 ml (1 fl oz) liquid glucose (optional)

80 g (2¾ oz) unsalted butter

banana cake with caramel sauce

serves 16

At home, if there are too many ripe bananas in the fruit bowl they usually end up in this cake. If time allows, make the caramel sauce and pour over the cake, however the cake is fine to eat on its own. The recipe for the caramel sauce is more than enough for the cake (making a smaller amount can become quite difficult without burning) and will keep in the refrigerator for at least 1 week — it also makes a great topping for ice cream. At Bourke Street Bakery we also use the caramel as a base in the chocolate tart. Warm it over low heat to bring it back to pouring consistency after refrigeration. The addition of glucose syrup helps to stop the sugar crystallising, but it is optional.

method

Preheat the oven to 200°C (400°F/Gas 6). Grease a 28 cm (11¼ inch) round cake tin and line the base and side with baking paper — the paper should protrude about 2.5 cm (1 inch) above the tin.

Put the butter and caster sugar in the bowl of an electric mixer fitted with a whisk attachment, and scrape in the vanilla seeds. Whisk on low speed until pale and creamy. Add the eggs one at a time, allowing each to be completely incorporated before adding more. Add the sour cream in two batches, then add the flour in two batches until combined.

Lightly mash the bananas and drizzle with golden syrup or sprinkle with brown sugar. Fold the mashed banana lightly through the cake mixture to combine, then spoon into the tin. Bake for 55 minutes to 1 hour 15 minutes, or until a skewer comes out clean when inserted into the centre of the cake. Cover the top of the cake loosely with baking paper if it starts to brown.

Meanwhile, to make the caramel sauce, pour the cream into a saucepan over high heat and bring it almost to boiling point.

Put the water, sugar and glucose syrup, if using, in a large saucepan over high heat and stir until the sugar dissolves. Once the sugar has dissolved, do not stir and cook for about 7–10 minutes, or until the liquid is a caramel colour. Remove from the heat (it will still go a little darker, so take care not to let it get too dark before removing it from the heat).

Pour the hot cream into the pan with the caramel, being careful, as the mixture will bubble up the side of the saucepan to about four times its original volume. Place it back on the heat and whisk until smooth. Remove from the heat, cool a little, then whisk in the butter.

Remove the cake from the oven and allow to cool for about 10 minutes, then remove from the tin and place on a large platter. To serve poke about forty holes into the cake using a skewer and pour the caramel sauce over the top while the cake is still warm.

ingredients

260 g (9¼ oz) dark chocolate (55% cocoa), finely chopped

135 ml (4½ fl oz) milk

40 g (½ oz) yoghurt

4 eggs

105 g (3¾ oz) caster (superfine) sugar, for eggs

4 egg whites

160 g (5¾ oz) caster (superfine) sugar, for egg whites

135 ml (4½ fl oz) pouring (whipping) cream (35% fat)

55 g (2 oz) unsweetened cocoa powder, sifted

This is a great cake — it is basically a cooked mousse, it puffs up high during cooking and collapses once removed from the oven to form a dense centre. It's best eaten within 4 hours of baking, as the top remains crisp during this time, adding another delicious texture to the cake. The beauty of this cake, and any other chocolate products for that matter, is that short of burning them you will end up with an acceptable product even if something goes wrong.

flourless chocolate cake

serves 12

method

Preheat the oven to 150°C (300°F/Gas 2). Grease a 20 cm (8 inch) spring-form cake tin and line the base and sides with baking paper — the paper should protrude about 2.5 cm (1 inch) above the tin.

Put the chocolate in a large stainless steel bowl and set over a saucepan of simmering water, making sure the base of the bowl does not touch the water — the bowl must be large enough to hold the whole cake mix. Allow the water in the saucepan to boil for 2 minutes, then turn off the heat and stir the chocolate while it slowly melts.

Put the milk and yoghurt in a saucepan over medium–high heat and bring to the boil. Turn off the heat — you should have a curdled milk mixture.

Put the eggs and the sugar for the eggs in the bowl of an electric mixer fitted with a whisk attachment. Whisk the eggs at medium speed for about 10 minutes, or until the mixture is very light and has doubled in volume.

In a very clean bowl, whisk the egg whites to soft peaks, then slowly add the sugar for the whites, whisking until soft peaks form a shiny meringue. Be careful not to overwhisk. Place in the refrigerator.

Whisk the cream until soft peaks form and place in the refrigerator until needed.

You should have ready to fold together the melted chocolate, curdled milk, whipped eggs, meringue, whipped cream and cocoa powder. Pour the curdled milk into the chocolate and use a whisk to mix it in, then add the cocoa and whisk to completely incorporate. Fold in the whipped eggs in three batches, making sure you completely incorporate the first batch before adding more — do not worry too much if you can still see streaks of eggs with the following batches. Lightly fold the meringue into the whipped cream, taking care not to knock out too much air. Fold this into the chocolate mix in three batches, making sure you incorporate the first batch before adding more.

Using a spatula, scoop the cake batter into the prepared tin and tap it twice gently on the bench to even out the mix. Bake for 1 hour 15 minutes to 1 hour 30 minutes. (If you can smell the cake cooking within the first 25 minutes your oven is too hot and you need to drop the temperature.) Do not disturb the cake for the first 45 minutes of cooking, after which time you should rotate it to ensure even cooking. You may need to cover the top of the cake with baking paper and lower the oven temperature if the top of the cake is starting to brown. Test to see if the cake is baked by gently placing your hand on top of it and wobbling it a little, you should feel that the cake has set through. Remove from the oven and allow to cool for about 30 minutes in the tin before removing the sides. When completely cool, slide the cake onto a serving plate, to serve.

It is best to use a sharp fine-bladed knife to cut this cake. Have a jug of very hot water, dip the knife in, and leave for about 10 seconds to warm the blade through. Dry the knife on a tea towel (dish towel) before slicing. Repeat this process after every slice for a perfectly clean cut.

note

This chocolate cake can be stored in an airtight container at room temperature for 1–2 days, and can be refrigerated for up to 5 days. Bring it back to room temperature for at least 2 hours before eating, or better still, warm it up in a 150°C (300°F/Gas 2) oven for about 10 minutes to freshen it up again. You can also enjoy this cake cut into portions and steamed for about 6–8 minutes, then topped with fresh berries and thick (double/heavy) cream.

ingredients

150 g (5½ oz/1½ cups) ground almonds

90 g (3¼ oz) plain (all-purpose) flour

240 g (8¾ oz) icing (confectioners') sugar, sifted

1 teaspoon baking powder

280 ml (9¾ fl oz/about 8) egg whites

250 g (9 oz) unsalted butter, melted

6 strawberries, hulled and halved

These little almond cakes, also known as friands, used to be baked ready for opening time each morning for customers to enjoy with a morning coffee — they make a fine morning tea cake or can be made in tiny ramekins as petits fours. Top them with a single piece of seasonal fruit, such as strawberry, blueberry, raspberry, mango or kiwi fruit. It's possible to substitute half of the ground almonds with ground coconut or ground pistachios to add a different flavour and texture. Should you have any left-over batter, it will keep in the refrigerator for about 3 days.

financiers with strawberry

makes 12

method

Preheat the oven to 190°C (375°F/Gas 5). Lightly grease a standard ½ cup 12-hole muffin tin with butter.

Put the ground almonds, flour, icing sugar and baking powder into a large mixing bowl. Add the egg whites, a little at a time, whisking well after each addition. Pour in the melted butter and whisk through until just combined.

Spoon the mixture into the holes in the prepared tin until they are almost full. Gently place a strawberry half into the top of each financier. Bake in the oven for about 30 minutes, or until they are golden and a skewer inserted into the centre comes out clean. Turn out onto a wire rack to cool and serve.

ingredients

400 g (14 oz/2⅔ cups) plain (all-purpose) flour	3 eggs
2 teaspoons baking powder	150 g (5½ oz/1 cup) strawberries, hulled and sliced
300 g (10½ oz) caster (superfine) sugar	150 g (5½ oz) raspberries
310 g (11 oz) unsalted butter	150 g (5½ oz) blueberries
480 ml (16¾ fl oz) buttermilk	30 g (1 oz) raw (demerara) sugar

Are these really muffins? Some purists say not, as a muffin usually has less sugar and uses vegetable oil instead of butter. These muffins also have a very low flour to butter ratio, resulting in what some customers have described as a pudding-like texture. Muffin or not, they are a very popular breakfast treat for those with a sweet tooth. The possible combinations of fruits for the muffins are endless, just use a little imagination and shop for fruit that's in season.

mixed berry muffins makes 12

method

Preheat the oven to 190°C (375°F/Gas 5). Lightly grease two large 6-hole muffin tins and line with paper cases.

Sift the flour and baking powder into a large bowl and add the sugar, mixing well to combine.

Melt the butter in a saucepan over medium heat, then remove from the heat and stir in the buttermilk. Using a whisk, stir in the eggs to combine. Pour over the dry ingredients and whisk to combine — don't worry if there are still some lumps of flour at this stage. Use a large spoon to gently fold through the fruit.

Spoon the mixture into the prepared muffin holes until almost full. Sprinkle the tops with the raw sugar. Reduce the oven temperature to 180°C (350°F/Gas 4) and bake for 25–30 minutes. It may be necessary to drop the temperature about 10 minutes before the end of baking time if the muffins are starting to brown on top. To test if the muffins are done, push the top gently to feel that it is firm and turn one out of the tray and see that the bottom has coloured. Remove from the oven and allow to cool in the tins for 10 minutes, before turning out onto a wire rack to cool completely.

ingredients

400 g (14 oz/2⅔ cups) plain (all-purpose) flour

2 teaspoons baking powder

300 g (10½ oz) caster (superfine) sugar

310 g (11 oz) unsalted butter

480 ml (16¾ fl oz) buttermilk

3 eggs

225 g (8 oz) dark chocolate (55% cocoa), roughly chopped

225 g (8 oz) raspberries, washed

55 g (2 oz/¼ cup) raw (demerara) sugar

icing (confectioners') sugar. for dusting

These are the most popular muffins sold at Bourke Street Bakery. Warm from the oven when the chocolate is still soft these muffins are a real treat.

dark chocolate and raspberry muffins

makes 12

method

Preheat the oven to 190°C (375°F/Gas 5). Lightly grease two large 6-hole muffin tins and line with paper cases.

Sift the flour and baking powder into a bowl and add the sugar, mixing well to combine.

Melt the butter in a saucepan over low heat, then remove from the heat and stir in the buttermilk. Using a whisk, stir in the eggs to combine. Pour over the dry ingredients and whisk to combine — don't worry if there are still some lumps of flour at this stage. Use a large spoon to gently fold through the chocolate and raspberries.

Spoon the mixture into the prepared muffin holes. Sprinkle the tops with the raw sugar. Reduce the oven temperature to 180°C (350°F/Gas 4) and bake for 25–30 minutes. It may be necessary to drop the temperature about 10 minutes before the end of baking time if the muffins are starting to brown on top. To test if the muffins are done, push the top gently to feel that it is firm and turn one out of the tray and see that the bottom has coloured. Remove from the oven and allow to cool in the tins for 10 minutes, before eating. Dust with icing sugar to serve.

ingredients

300 g (10½ oz/1⅓ cups) pitted prunes, halved

200 ml (7 fl oz) brandy, cognac or hot black tea

55 g (2 oz) plain (all-purpose) flour

40 g (1½ oz/⅓ cup) unsweetened cocoa powder

¼ teaspoon salt

2 teaspoons baking powder

300 g (10½ oz) good-quality dark chocolate (55% cocoa)

80 g (2¾ oz) unsalted butter

300 g (10½ oz) caster (superfine) sugar

4 eggs

100 g (3½ oz) sour cream

145 g (5¼ oz/1 cup) dark chocolate melts (buttons) (55% cocoa)

This rich brownie is made extra moist by the alcohol-soaked prunes, which you will need to soak for 3 days before. If you prefer, the alcohol can be replaced with tea, which adds a wonderful flavour to the prunes. The prunes can be replaced with dried fruit or nuts if you like.

chocolate prune brownie makes 32

method

Place the prunes in a bowl and pour over the brandy, cognac or tea. Cover and set aside to soak for 3 days.

Preheat the oven to 170°C (325°F/Gas 3). Grease a 20 x 30 x 4 cm (8 x 12 x 1½ inch) rectangular cake tin and line the base and sides with baking paper. Sift the flour, cocoa, salt and baking powder into a bowl.

Put the chocolate, butter and sugar into a stainless steel bowl and sit over a saucepan of simmering water — making sure the base of the bowl does not touch the water. Stir for 10 minutes, or until the chocolate has melted. Allow to cool, then transfer to the bowl of an electric mixer fitted with a paddle attachment. Mix on medium speed and add the eggs, one at a time, beating well after each addition. Add the flour mixture, mix to combine, then add the sour cream, chocolate melts and prunes with the remaining soaking liquid and mix until just combined.

Spoon the mixture into the prepared tin and bake in the oven for 1 hour, or until just set. Place your hand on top of the brownie in the centre and wobble to feel if it is set. Allow to cool completely before turning out of the tin. Use a hot knife to cut into squares. The brownies can be wrapped in plastic wrap and stored for up to 4 days at room temperature.

ingredients

1.125 kg (2 lb 7 oz/7$\frac{1}{2}$ cups) plain (all-purpose) flour

5 g ($\frac{1}{8}$ oz/1 teaspoon) salt

5 g ($\frac{1}{8}$ oz/1 teaspoon) bicarbonate of soda (baking soda)

15 g ($\frac{1}{2}$ oz/1$\frac{1}{2}$ tablespoons) ground ginger

5 g ($\frac{1}{8}$ oz/2 teaspoons) ground cinnamon

5 g ($\frac{1}{8}$ oz/2 teaspoons) ground nutmeg

400 g (14 oz) unsalted butter

400 g (14 oz) soft brown sugar

320 g (11$\frac{1}{4}$ oz) golden syrup or honey

1 egg

4 egg yolks

royal icing

250 g (9 oz/2 cups) icing (confectioners') sugar

1 egg white

$\frac{1}{2}$ teaspoon freshly squeezed lemon juice

gingerbread biscuits

makes 48 biscuits

Gingerbread biscuits are great for kids to cut into different shapes and decorate with royal icing and lollies (candies). They can also be used to make gingerbread houses. Cut the pieces to size before baking and don't roll them out too thinly or they will become quite fragile after baking. Construct the house on a firm base and use the royal icing to glue it together.

method

Preheat the oven to 170°C (325°F/Gas 3). To make the biscuits, sift the flour, salt, bicarbonate of soda and spices together into a large bowl.

Put the butter, sugar and golden syrup in a large bowl and mix with hand-held electric beaters on medium speed until pale and creamy. Add the egg and egg yolks in a slow stream and mix until well combined. Add the dry ingredients, in three batches, until thoroughly mixed through. Divide the dough into four even-sized portions and flatten each portion into a disc. Cover in plastic wrap and refrigerate for at least 20 minutes, or for up to 3 days.

Remove from the refrigerator and allow the dough to soften slightly. Roll out each disc between two sheets of baking paper until about 3 mm (1/8 inch) thick. Cut into the desired shapes using biscuit cutters or a knife. Re-roll to make use of all the dough.

Place the biscuits on baking trays lined with baking paper and bake, in batches, for 15–20 minutes, or until slightly puffed and golden. Allow to cool on the trays.

Meanwhile, make the royal icing. Sift the icing sugar through a fine sieve. Place the egg white in a bowl and add 1 tablespoon of the icing sugar. Using a wooden spoon, beat to form a smooth paste, then keep adding the sugar, 1 tablespoon at a time, beating well after each addition. Stir in the lemon juice — you should be able to squeeze the mixture through a piping (icing) bag. The icing can be divided into smaller batches and a few drops of food colouring can be added if required. Place the icing in a piping (icing) bag fitted with a fine nozzle and pipe the desired shapes on the biscuits. The biscuits can be eaten when the icing hardens, or stored in an airtight container for up to 2 weeks.

ingredients

175 g (6 oz) unsalted butter

250 g (9 oz/1²⁄₃ cups) plain (all-purpose) flour

60 g (2¼ oz/⅓ cup) rice flour

1 teaspoon baking powder

½ teaspoon salt

125 g (4½ oz) caster (superfine) sugar

80 g (2¾ oz/½ cup) macadamia nuts, chopped

This a very buttery shortbread. Any nuts can be substituted for the macadamias, or the nuts can be omitted for a plain shortbread. Be careful not to get too much colour when baking, shortbread should be light golden.

macadamia shortbread

makes 16

method

Preheat the oven to 180°C (350°F/Gas 4). Line a 20 cm (8 inch) square slice tin, about 4 cm (1½ inch) deep, with baking paper.

Remove the butter from the refrigerator 20 minutes before using. Sift the plain flour, rice flour, baking powder and salt into a bowl. Add the caster sugar and stir to combine.

Cut the butter into 1.5 cm (⅝ inch) cubes and use your fingertips to gently rub the butter into the dry ingredients, until the mixture resembles breadcrumbs. Add the macadamias and continue rubbing together to combine, and then knead to form a dough.

Pat the mixture into the prepared tin and smooth the top using the back of a spoon, making sure it is even all over. Place in the refrigerator for 20 minutes to rest.

Bake in the oven for 30–40 minutes, or until the shortbread is light golden and firm to the touch. Allow to cool in the tin before turning out and cutting into fingers with a serrated knife. Shortbread can be stored in an airtight container for up to 5 days.

ingredients

Christmas Fruit Soak
(make the fruit soak 5 weeks in advance)

55 g (2 oz/¼ cup) caster (superfine) sugar

55 ml (1¾ fl oz) water

160 ml (5¼ fl oz) brandy

90 g (3¼ oz/¾ cup) sultanas (golden raisins)

80 g (2¾ oz/½ cup) currants

80 g (2¾ oz/⅓ cup) pitted prunes, chopped

80 g (2¾ oz/½ cup) fresh pitted dates, chopped

150 g (5½ oz/1¼ cups) raisins

55 g (2 oz/⅓ cup) mixed peel (mixed candied citrus peel)

135 g (4¾ oz/¾ cup) chopped dried figs

cake

100 g (3½ oz/⅔ cup) plain (all-purpose) flour

½ teaspoon mixed (pumpkin pie) spice

15 g (½ oz) ground almonds

110 g (3¾ oz) unsalted butter

100 g (3½ oz) soft brown sugar

2 teaspoons honey

2 tablespoons treacle

1 teaspoon marmalade

3 eggs, lightly beaten

150 ml (5 fl oz) brandy, for feeding

brandy butter

200 g (7 oz) unsalted butter, softened

125 g (4½ oz/1 cup) icing (confectioners') sugar, sifted

60 ml (2 fl oz/¼ cup) brandy

bourke street bakery
christmas cake serves 12–16

method

To make the fruit soak, put the sugar in a saucepan with the water and bring to the boil over high heat, stirring to dissolve the sugar. Remove from the heat and allow to cool. Pour the brandy and cooled sugar syrup into an airtight container and add the fruit, mixing well to coat. Cover and keep at room temperature for about 5 weeks. During the first week you will need to stir the fruit daily; for the following four weeks you will only need to stir the fruit once a week — you should be left with a thick syrupy fruit mix. If you're not ready to make the cake at this time, refrigerate the fruit for up to 2 months — it will only get better.

When you are ready to make the cake, preheat the oven to 190°C (375°F/ Gas 5). Grease two 12.5 cm (4¾ inch) round cake tins and line the base and side of each tin with baking paper.

Sift the flour, mixed spice and ground almonds together in a bowl. In the bowl of an electric mixer fitted with a paddle attachment, cream the butter, sugar, honey, treacle and marmalade, until pale. Add the eggs, a little at a time, ensuring each amount is completely incorporated before adding more — take care the mixture doesn't curdle at this stage — if you see it starting to separate slightly, add a small amount of the flour mix to bring it back together. With the motor still running, add the flour — stop as soon as it is combined. Using a gloved hand fold in 900 g (2 lb) of the fruit soak, until combined.

Divide the mixture evenly between the prepared cake tins, tapping heavily on the bench to settle. Place the cake tins on an oven tray and place in the oven. Immediately lower the temperature to 160°C (315°F/ Gas 2–3) and bake for about 40 minutes. Turn the tray and bake for 20 minutes further. The cakes are cooked when a skewer inserted into the centre of each cake comes out clean. It may take up to 1 hour 20 minutes to bake — cover the top of the cake loosely with baking paper if the top starts to brown. Remove from the oven and leave in the tins to cool.

Make about 20–30 holes in each cake using a skewer, and pushing it about three-quarters of the way through the cake. Cut two large sheets of foil and two large sheets of baking paper. Place each piece of foil on the bench and lay a sheet of baking paper over each. Working with one cake at a time, place the cake on the baking paper and draw the paper and foil up around the cake scrunching it together on top to form a container that will hold any alcohol, which may soak through when feeding the cakes. Repeat with the remaining cake.

To feed the cakes, open up the top of the foil wrapping and brush over about 1 teaspoon of brandy. Repeat this every 3–4 days for 8–10 weeks or until the alcohol seems not to be soaking in anymore. Be sure the foil is well closed after each feed to stop evaporation, which will lead to the cakes drying out. It's best to keep the cakes in an airtight container to keep ants or any little critters that like cake (and alcohol) at bay. Once the cakes are fed, wrap them very well and store them in the container in a dark cool place until ready to serve.

To make the brandy butter, put the butter and icing sugar in the bowl of an electric mixer fitted with a whisk attachment. Cream the butter and sugar on medium speed until pale and fluffy. With the motor still running, gradually pour in the brandy, making sure it disappears into the mix as it is added. Once all the brandy is incorporated, transfer to an airtight container and refrigerate. The butter will keep for 2 weeks in the refrigerator. Serve the brandy butter at room temperature.

The Bourke Street Bakery Christmas cakes are individually hand-wrapped in calico and tied with twine, ready to be displayed and sold for the few weeks leading up to Christmas. We make smallish cakes as they are very rich and after an indulgent Christmas lunch or dinner, small portions are generally best. These cakes also bake very slowly – to make larger cakes the tins need to be lined with layers of brown paper to stop the sides burning. This recipe allows for two smaller cakes but can easily be doubled or tripled, as long as you have a mixer large enough to handle the increased volumes.

This is a dense cake that is rich in fruit. Like all good fruit cakes it needs to be made a few months in advance and after baking it needs to be soaked with alcohol every 3–4 days for up to 10 weeks. These cakes can be heated in a steamer or microwave and eaten warm like a pudding, served with brandy butter. You can make the brandy butter a few weeks ahead to lighten your load on the big day.

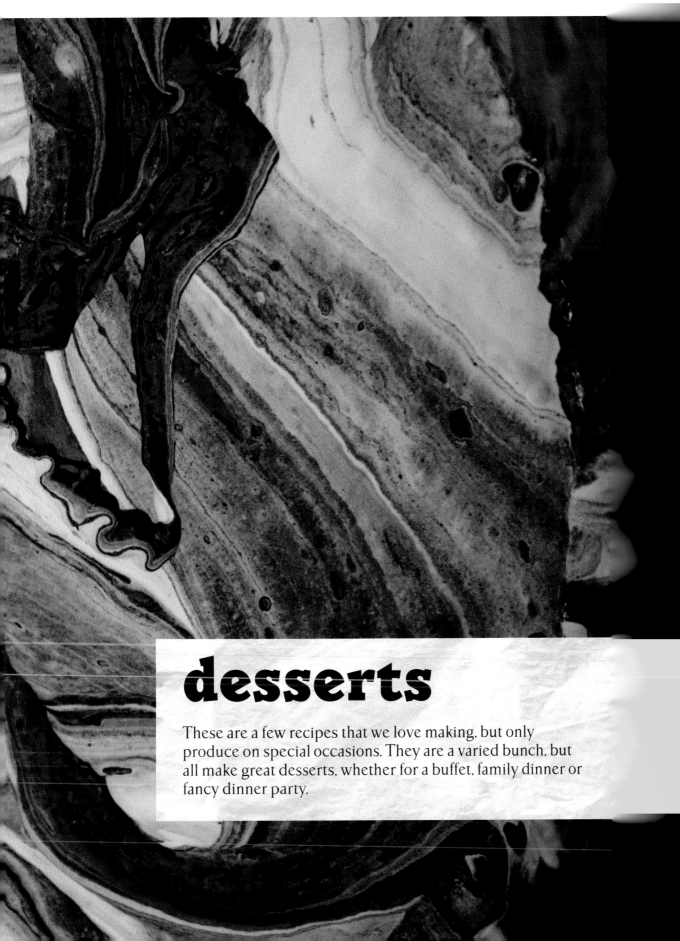

desserts

These are a few recipes that we love making, but only produce on special occasions. They are a varied bunch, but all make great desserts, whether for a buffet, family dinner or fancy dinner party.

105 g (3¾ oz/about 3) egg whites
210 g (7½ oz) caster (superfine) sugar

At Bourke Street Bakery we have found that the Swiss meringue is the best individual soft-centred meringue. The basic recipe we use here is double the weight of sugar to egg whites — the meringue is first warmed in a bain marie to dissolve the sugar before whipping the egg whites to firm peaks. To add a little flavour, it is possible to sift a little unsweetened cocoa powder over the meringue, or use a squeeze bottle (similar to one used for tomato sauce) to squirt squiggles of puréed raspberries, strawberries or any fruit that takes your fancy, just before placing in the oven.

meringues

makes 12–18 small, or 4–6 large, meringues

method

Preheat the oven to 130°C (250°F/Gas 1). In a very clean stainless steel bowl stir together the egg white and sugar. Place the bowl over a saucepan of boiling water and continue stirring, regularly scraping down the side of the bowl with a rubber spatula to ensure no sugar crystals form. Once all the sugar has dissolved and you have a smooth, clear, warm liquid, remove from the heat — wipe the bottom of the bowl to ensure no water can come into contact with the mix.

Transfer the warm liquid to the clean bowl of an electric mixer fitted with a whisk attachment. Beat for about 10 minutes on high speed, or until the mixture is cool and firm peaks have formed.

Spoon or pipe the meringue into the desired shape directly onto the baking trays lined with baking paper. Lower the oven temperature to 100°C (200°F/Gas ½) and bake for about 1 hour 30 minutes, or until crisp on the outside and soft in the centre. If you prefer a dry meringue you can cook them for up to 6 hours. The best way to test if the meringue is ready is to break one open — a soft meringue should have a crisp shell and the centre should be set like a marshmallow and warm all the way through when first removed from the oven. The cooking time will vary quite substantially for meringues of different sizes. Remove from the oven and cool on wire racks. The meringues can be eaten when cool, or stored in airtight container for up to 2–3 days.

variation

Chocolate meringues are a favourite of many children and adults alike. At Bourke Street Bakery we only bake them if we can fit them into the schedule, or if we have egg whites left-over from another dish — often we go six months between bakes and the protests are quite loud and continuous at these times.

Once you have prepared the meringue mixture above, sift 100 g (3½ oz) unsweetened cocoa powder into a large bowl. Using a large serving spoon, scoop out meringues a little larger than a tennis ball and drop into the cocoa. Working with one ball at a time, swill the bowl to make the meringue roll like a ball and completely coat it with cocoa. Gently lift the meringue out and place it on a baking tray lined with baking paper. Repeat with the remaining meringue to make up to six in total. Gently dig the tips of your fingers into the meringue and drag them upwards, creating streaks of white and chocolate meringue. Bake at 100°C (200°F/Gas ½) for about 1 hour 30 minutes, or until crisp on the outside and soft in the centre.

tips for making successful meringues

- To get the best results you really need to make sure that all your equipment is spotlessly clean, dry and free of grease before you start. After carefully washing all bowls and mixing implements they can be wiped down with some lemon juice to help remove any residual grease, then dry them well.
- Be very careful when separating the eggs as the tiniest scrap of egg yolk in the whites will stop the meringue reaching its full volume or in the worst case, can stop it from gaining any volume at all.
- Mixing the ingredients in a copper bowl, if you have one, can help to add volume to the meringue and helps the meringue hold its volume.
- High humidity in the kitchen can adversely affect the meringue. It is best not to let the meringue sit in the bowl too long after mixing — divide into desired portions and immediately place in the oven.

ingredients

meringue

4 egg whites

250 g (9 oz) caster (superfine) sugar

⅓ teaspoon natural vanilla extract

⅓ teaspoon white vinegar

mascarpone filling

2 egg whites

25 g (1 oz) caster (superfine) sugar, for egg whites

2 egg yolks

35 g (1¼ oz) caster (superfine) sugar, for egg yolks

500 g (1 lb 2 oz) mascarpone cheese

2–3 ripe mangoes,

125 ml (4 fl oz) passionfruit pulp

layered passionfruit and mango meringue

serves 10

This dessert is a play on the classic pavlova and the Italian tiramisu. In the Bourke Street Bakery version, meringue sheets replace the savoiardi (lady finger) biscuits of a traditional tiramisu, and are layered with mascarpone and fresh mango slices and passionfruit. The finished product can be served buffet-style and simply scooped out of its dish with a large serving spoon. For a more formal occasion it can be made in a 30 cm (12 inch) spring-form cake tin and carefully cut into portions and served as a plated dessert.

method

Preheat the oven to 140°C (275°F/Gas 1). Line three 30 x 20 cm (12 x 8 inch) baking trays with baking paper.

To make the meringues, put the egg whites into the very clean bowl of an electric mixer fitted with a whisk attachment. Whisk the egg whites on high speed until firm peaks form. With the motor still running, slowly pour in the sugar and whisk until shiny, firm peaks form. Use a rubber spatula to fold through the vanilla extract and vinegar. Scoop the meringue onto the three trays and use a palette knife to quickly spread the meringue evenly over each tray. Bake for 20–25 minutes, or until just starting to take on some colour. Remove from the oven and allow to cool on the trays. Run a knife around the edge to release the meringue, turn out and cool.

To make the mascarpone filling, put the egg whites in the very clean bowl of an electric mixer fitted with a whisk attachment. Mix the egg whites on high speed until soft peaks form. With the motor still running, slowly pour in the sugar for the whites and mix until soft peaks form — be careful not to overmix. Transfer to a bowl and refrigerate until needed.

Put the egg yolks and the sugar for the yolks into the cleaned mixing bowl and use the whisk attachment to combine on medium speed. Add the mascarpone and continue mixing for about 30 seconds, or until it becomes quite smooth. Remove the bowl from the mixer and fold in the chilled meringue in two batches, being careful not to overwork and knock out all the air.

Peel the mangoes and cut into slices about 5 mm (¼ inch) thick. Place a sheet of the cooked meringue into a 20 x 30 x 6 cm (8 x 12 x 2½ inch) ceramic baking dish, trimming the sheets slightly to fit if needed. Place half of the mascarpone filling over the meringue and spread evenly with a palette knife, making sure you spread it all the way to the edges. Arrange with a single layer of sliced mangoes and half of the passionfruit pulp. Place another meringue sheet on top, spread with the remaining mascarpone and then arrange the remaining mango and passionfruit over the top. Finally, top with the last meringue sheet. Refrigerate for at least 4–6 hours, or until set.

variation

There are endless combinations of fruits that could be used in this cake. We have also used rhubarb, which has been roasted in the oven with a sprinkling of sugar, as well as fresh peaches, which are fantastic in season. It's also possible to fold some desiccated coconut or ground almonds through the meringue.

pear jelly

15 x 2 g (¹/₁₆ oz) gelatine leaves or
1¹/₂ tablespoons powdered gelatine

600 ml (21 fl oz) pear poaching liquid
(see page 188)

500 ml (17 fl oz/2 cups) water

orange jelly

18 x 2 g (¹/₁₆ oz) gelatine leaves or
2¹/₄ tablespoons powdered gelatine

800 ml (28 fl oz) freshly squeezed
orange juice, strained

200 ml (7 fl oz) water

200 g (7 oz) caster (superfine)
sugar

crème anglaise

750 ml (26 fl oz/3 cups) milk

200 g (7 oz) caster (superfine) sugar

1 vanilla bean, split lengthways

9 egg yolks, lightly beaten

1 layer sponge cake (see page 311)

185 ml (6 fl oz/³/₄ cup) sherry

4 peaches, stones removed and
cut into eighths

250 g (9 oz) strawberries, hulled
and halved

peach and strawberry trifle

serves 10

The crème anglaise used in this trifle is a pouring custard about the same consistency as pouring cream, although it ends up as more of a sloppy mess than the set trifles most people are used to. Crème anglaise is also perfect served warm or cold and poured over fresh seasonal fruit. It is an excellent accompaniment for the flourless chocolate cake on pages 318–19. If you plan to take the trifle to a picnic you should use the crème pâttissière (see pages 276–7) as it sets firmer. It would even be possible to use the vanilla lime pannacotta (see pages 286–7) as a substitute for custard. If you use the crème pâtissière or pannacotta, pour them over the trifle before they have set.

method

To make the pear jelly, soak the gelatine leaves in a large container of cold water for 2–3 minutes, to soften. If using powdered gelatine, place in a bowl with 100 ml ($3^1/_2$ fl oz) of the water and stir to dissolve. Put the pear poaching liquid and water in a saucepan over medium heat and bring to the boil, skimming off any impurities that rise to the surface. Remove from the heat. Lift the gelatine leaves from the water, squeezing out any excess water, then drop them into the hot pear syrup and stir to dissolve. If using powdered gelatine, add the gelatine mixture to the hot syrup and stir to dissolve. Strain the mixture through a fine sieve. Set aside to cool. Pour into a bowl and refrigerate overnight to set.

To make the orange jelly, soak the gelatine leaves in a large container of cold water for 2–3 minutes, to soften. If using powdered gelatine, place in a bowl with 100 ml ($3^1/_2$ fl oz) of the water and stir to combine. Put the water and sugar in a saucepan over medium heat and bring to the boil, stirring to dissolve the sugar, remove from the heat as soon as it boils. Lift the gelatine leaves from the water, squeezing out any excess water, then drop them into the hot sugar syrup and stir to dissolve. If using powdered gelatine, add the gelatine mixture to the hot syrup and stir to dissolve. Strain the mixture through a fine sieve. Set aside to cool slightly, then stir in the orange juice. Pour into a bowl and refrigerate overnight to set.

To make the crème anglaise, put the milk and sugar in a saucepan over medium heat. Scrape the vanilla seeds from the bean and add the seeds and bean to the pan. Stir until almost boiling to dissolve the sugar, then remove from the heat.

Pour the warm milk mixture into a bowl with the lightly beaten egg yolks and whisk well to combine. Pour this mixture back into the saucepan over low–medium heat, stirring continuously with a wooden spoon for 8–12 minutes, or until the custard thickens slightly — be careful not to boil the custard or it will curdle. The common test to see if the custard is cooked in a professional kitchen is to lift the spoon from the custard and run your finger along the back of the spoon; if the line made by your finger remains clear the custard is cooked. Pour the custard through a fine sieve and whisk for a few minutes to cool. Cover with plastic wrap and refrigerate until needed.

To assemble the trifle, cut the sponge cake into 3-4 cm ($1^1/_4$–$1^1/_2$ inch) cubes and place in a large serving bowl. Sprinkle the sherry over the cake. Scatter over the combined fruit. Cut the jellies into 2–3 cm ($^3/_4$–$1^1/_4$ inch) cubes and scatter over the cake and fruit. Pour half the crème anglaise over the top and place in the refrigerator for about 2 hours to allow the custard to soak through. Serve with the extra crème anglaise passed around in a jug.

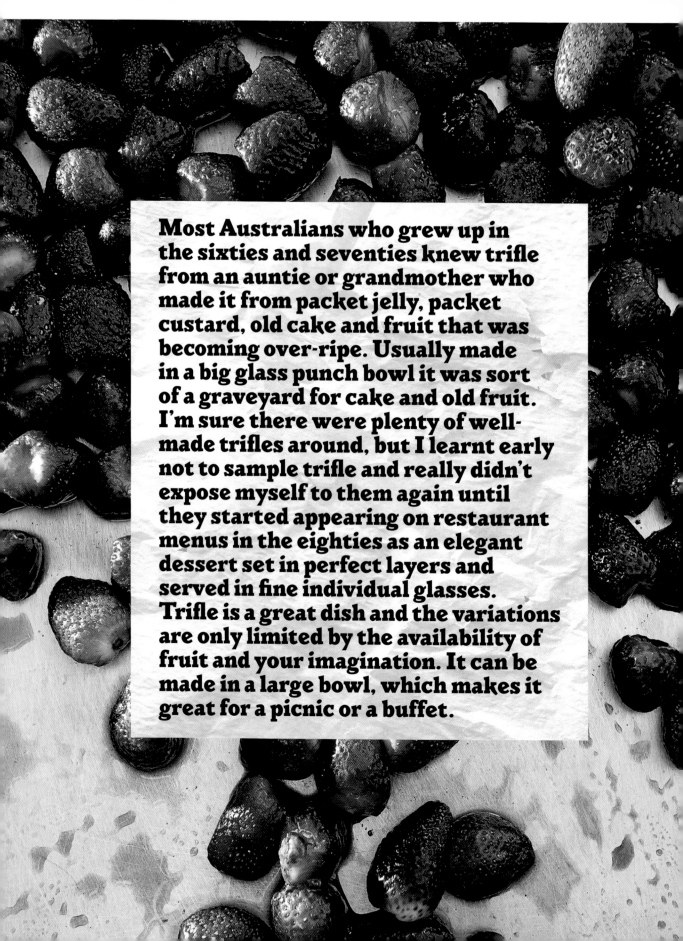

Most Australians who grew up in the sixties and seventies knew trifle from an auntie or grandmother who made it from packet jelly, packet custard, old cake and fruit that was becoming over-ripe. Usually made in a big glass punch bowl it was sort of a graveyard for cake and old fruit. I'm sure there were plenty of well-made trifles around, but I learnt early not to sample trifle and really didn't expose myself to them again until they started appearing on restaurant menus in the eighties as an elegant dessert set in perfect layers and served in fine individual glasses. Trifle is a great dish and the variations are only limited by the availability of fruit and your imagination. It can be made in a large bowl, which makes it great for a picnic or a buffet.

index

acknowledgments

Firstly, thank you to our stalwart staff: Mary, the best croissant maker in the force; Nadine, for sharing many recipes in the early days; Cleggy, for the emails; Kearns, don't eat the chocolate; Dan Zanello, I'm just a squirrel looking for a nut; Katrina, be there at 4 am; Giddo, I only work Fridays; Ji, the best croissant maker beyond the force; Cibej, clean our windows; Cooper, do I own the bakery? Thanks also to our indomitable managers Rob and Ren; Jason Warwick, you've taught us so much about baking; Val, without you this would all be one big mess; to all staff past and present; to our tradesmen, designers and suppliers, thank you for your quality.

Thanks to the team at Murdoch Books for helping make this book happen.

Paul

We think of Bourke Street Bakery as a community bakery. So many people in the neighbourhood are involved in its success in small but significant ways. So to all of you who help and organise, socialise and suggest, queue patiently while eating sausage rolls and drinking coffee – we thank you. It is you that has put the bakery on the map and made this book possible.

I must thank a few of the main players. Firstly, my parents, who get up at the crack of dawn each week to travel to Flemington to source the best fruit and vegies, and who are also responsible for the flower arrangements. I love that you are involved with the bakery and can not thank you enough. To my wife, Jessica, the brightest spark in my life. I love my life with you. Thank you for your trust, commitment and belief in me. To our little boy Gideon who keeps everything in perspective, I never realised I could love a being so much.

Thank you to my old bosses Kim de Laive and Alex Herbert for teaching me that only the best will do; to my dedicated sub-editor, Katja Grynberg, this is a better book because of you. Thank you to my sister, Gabrielle, who in the early days always had time for design advice. Thank you also to Bob Grynberg, who is always a font of wisdom, generosity and good humour.

David

Thanks to Sam, my partner, the kindest most caring person I know. Thank you for being the bakery's strongest critic and proudest devotee. You bought three cups for the bakery kitchen staff as an opening day gift — one for me, one for Paul and one in case we ended up employing another staff member — we did. Our daughter Safina, thanks for coming into the world during the writing of this book. My life becomes so much greater every day because of you. My brother Rod, thank you for giving up your holidays to do the carpentry work at the first Bourke Street Bakery. Mum and Dad, there are no better parents than you. Thank you.

Jessica, thanks for the continuous work you do for the bakery in the background, it's greatly appreciated. To the Grynberg family, thank you for being so generous to the bakery from the moment the doors opened.

Published in 2009 by Murdoch Books Pty Limited

Murdoch Books Australia
Pier 8/9
23 Hickson Road
Millers Point NSW 2000
Phone: +61 (0) 2 8220 2000
Fax: +61 (0) 2 8220 2558
www.murdochbooks.com.au

Murdoch Books UK Limited
Erico House, 6th Floor
93–99 Upper Richmond Road
Putney, London SW15 2TG
Phone: +44 (0) 20 8785 5995
Fax: +44 (0) 20 8785 5985
www.murdochbooks.co.uk

Publisher: Jane Lawson
Project editor: Kristin Buesing
Editor: Jacqueline Blanchard
Designer: Hugh Ford
Photographer: Alan Benson
Stylist: Sarah O'Brien
Food editor: Sonia Greig
Production: Alexandra Gonzalez

National Library of Australia Cataloguing-in-Publication Data
Authors: Allam, Paul. Mcguinness, David
Title: Bourke Street Bakery
ISBN: 9781741964332 (hbk.)
Notes: Includes index.
Subjects: Baking.
Dewey Number: 641.71

A catalogue record for this book is available from the British Library.

Printed by 1010 Printing International Limited, China.
PRINTED IN CHINA. Reprinted 2009 (twice), 2010 (three times), 2011.

IMPORTANT: Those who might be at risk from the effects of salmonella poisoning (the elderly, pregnant women, young children and those suffering from immune deficiency diseases) should consult their doctor with any concerns about eating raw eggs.

OVEN GUIDE: You may find cooking times vary depending on the oven you are using. For fan-forced ovens, as a general rule, set the oven temperature to 20°C (35°F) lower than indicated in the recipe.